on track ...
Def Leppard

every album, every song

Scott Robinson

sonicbondpublishing.com

Sonicbond Publishing Limited
www.sonicbondpublishing.co.uk
Email: info@sonicbondpublishing.co.uk

First Published in the United Kingdom 2026
First Published in the United States 2026

British Library Cataloguing in Publication Data:
A Catalogue record for this book is available from the British Library

Typeset in ITC Garamond Std & ITC Avant Garde Gothic
Printed and bound in England

Graphic design and typesetting: Full Moon Media

Follow us on social media:
Twitter: https://twitter.com/SonicbondP
Instagram: www.instagram.com/sonicbondpublishing_/
Facebook: www.facebook.com/SonicbondPublishing/

Linktree QR code:

on track ...
Def Leppard

Contents

Origins: Sheffield, UK 5

The Def Leppard EP (1979) 7

On Through The Night (1980) 11

High 'N' Dry (1981) 21

Pyromania (1983) 30

Interim: 31 December 1984 39

Hysteria (1987) 41

Interim: 8 January 1991 56

Adrenalize (1992) 58

Retro Active (1993) 68

Slang (1996) 74

Euphoria (1999) 83

X (2002) 90

Yeah! (2006) 96

Songs From The Sparkle Lounge (2008) 103

Def Leppard (2015) 108

Diamond Star Halos (2022) 113

Live Albums 120

Compilations 123

Box Sets 127

Sources/Bibliography 128

For my son, Steve – Leppard's biggest fan

Origins: Sheffield, UK

North-Central England exudes a sense of romance across the landscape of rock history, owing, of course, to four lads from Liverpool. The Beatles got rock rolling in the early 1960s, but other voices would emerge in the working-class hinterlands, taking what the Fab Four had started in new directions.

Liverpool's other alumni included Gerry Marsden, who would front the Pacemakers, and Ian McCulloch, who would go on to found Echo & the Bunnymen more than a decade later. Elsewhere in the north, Graham Nash had grown up in Salford – just outside Manchester – where Liam and Noel Gallagher would one day create an Oasis.

And as the 1960s were becoming the 1970s, the steel town of Sheffield served up a coarse blues rocker named Joe Cocker, who infused The Beatles' bounciest pop with a soulful R&B wail – advancing the British innovation that, in rock, anything can be anything, and the further out, the better.

By the mid-1970s, that hybridisation had gone in unexpected directions, particularly with the aggressive mash-up of hard rock (Black Sabbath, Deep Purple) and glam (David Bowie, T. Rex), generating a new and exuberant genre, the New Wave of British Heavy Metal. Teenagers across the nation went all in on NWOBHM, scooping up Judas Priest and Iron Maiden, Motörhead and Saxon, Venom and Diamond Head.

And over in Cocker's Sheffield, rock was undergoing yet another mitosis, as young rockers were getting their hands on synthesisers and putting them where the guitars were supposed to go. As NWOBHM was rapidly surging, Sheffield was birthing The Human League and Cabaret Voltaire – the progenitors of British synthpop.

In Tapton, a secondary school in Sheffield's Crosspool, a handful of headbangers who had spent their formative years immersed in Thin Lizzy and Queen knew which of those new camps they wanted to be in.

One of those headbangers was Rick Savage, an aspiring rocker who industriously formed a garage band, Atomic Mass, with his pals Tony Kenning, a drummer, and Pete Willis, who played guitar. Savage – Sav to his friends – played bass, and a parade of lead singers and second guitarists (after the twin guitar model of TL, Judas Priest and Iron Maiden) came and went until the band found its missing ingredient – an in-your-face frontman who could pull off the kind of songs they had kicking around in their heads.

Guitarist Pete Willis found the guy. 'I knew this guy, Joe Elliott', he told *Rolling Stone*'s David Fricke. 'I'd seen him one or two times at a youth club, Columbus, in an area of Sheffield called Crosspool. His friend, Craig, was a friend of mine. Craig must have told Joe that I had an amplifier I was interested in selling. So, Joe turned up at my parents' house one day and said, 'I hear you've got an amplifier. I just bought a guitar and I was wondering if you'd be interested in selling that amplifier.' I thought, 'This guy's got cheek. He's got to be a good front man.' Atomic Mass now had its lead singer.

'I was awful,' Joe told the *Honolulu Advertiser,* 'but I was much better than the guy they had before. They liked me because I looked right. I was tall and I had long hair and I didn't look wimpy, like Elvis Costello and guys like that.' He also gave the band a new name – Deaf Leopard – which he came up with while doodling hypothetical album covers in school.

Finally, there was Steve Clark, who struck up a conversation with Willis when he saw him reading a guitar book at school. Willis, along with Elliott, persuaded Clark to audition – and the first band lineup was born.

Def Leppard was now complete and ready to rock.

The Def Leppard EP (1979)

Personnel:
Joe Elliott: lead and backing vocals
Rick Savage: bass, vocals
Steve Clark: lead guitar, vocals
Pete Willis: lead guitar, vocals
Frank Noon: drums
Recorded at Fairview Studios in November 1978
Producer: Def Leppard
Engineers: Keith Herd, Roy Neave
Released in January 1979
Label: Bludgeon Riffola Records
Sales: 2,500
Chart position: UK: 84 (BBC Singles chart)
Running time: 14:37

Every new band needs a calling card, something that will get their music out into the world. For the fledgling Deaf Leopard, that would be an EP – a short record with a handful of their songs.

It was in the planning of that EP that Deaf Leopard became Def Leppard, at the suggestion of Tony Kenning – his last official contribution to the band, as he was dismissed before recording began over his apparent lack of dedication (it was a girlfriend thing, and he would later call it 'the biggest regret of my life.'). Joe Elliott's friend Frank Noon took the drum chair for the session.

Joe's father, Phil Elliott, financed the session, loaning his son £150. 'My dad literally emptied out his bank account', he later said. 'That's how much faith he had in his son, God bless him. He didn't give me the money – he loaned it to me. But as he told me over a few whiskies in years gone by, had he had the opportunity to do what I was doing, he would have jumped at it, so he wasn't going to stop me.'

Three songs were recorded in the session, which took place over a November weekend. Backing tracks and solos were laid down on Saturday. Rick Savage remembered the moment they listened to themselves for the first time in a studio: 'My clearest memory is being in the control room and hearing a playback of the first ten seconds of 'Ride Into The Sun'. I thought, 'This sounds amazing!' It was such a rush of excitement – a feeling I'll never forget.'

Joe laid down his vocals that evening and the following morning. 'I was a bit tipsy on the Saturday night and really giving it some', he said. 'It was more difficult doing the scream in 'The Overture' on the Sunday morning. I felt really self-conscious. It didn't feel right, but we flooded my vocals in echo and it was okay.'

The bill for the session ended up being £148.50. They bought themselves some celebratory fish and chips with the change, he recalled in *Definitely: The Official Story Of Def Leppard*. 'We drove home listening to the cassette over and over again on the car stereo, going, 'We've done it, we've made a record!"

After the session, Frank Noon was offered a permanent spot in the band. But he declined, opting to remain loyal to the band he was already in. Rick Allen was hired the following week. He had just turned 15. 'Once we heard Rick play, we were blown away', Elliott said. 'It was a no-brainer.'

The EP was issued with the label Bludgeon Riffola Records – their own garage label relying on their own street corner distribution. Joe secured a loan of £450 from a coworker, money that went into pressing 1,000 copies of the EP. He and his mother folded the record sleeves together themselves, and he printed lyric sheets on a Xerox machine in the office where he worked. The band then set about selling copies one by one to anyone who would buy them, for £1 apiece.

Joe wasn't half bad as a promo man, slipping a copy to popular DJ John Peel, who gave it a listen and played it on BBC Radio 1. The initial pressing of 1,000 sold out quickly, giving them enough cash to do a second run of 1,500, which also sold out. Joe was easily able to repay the loans. 'We didn't make any money out of it,' Elliott said, 'but as a promotional exercise, you couldn't beat it.'

At the time, they had no idea just how effective *The Def Leppard EP* would be. It made its way to Mercury Records A&R man Cliff Burnstein, who loved it so much and believed in the band so strongly that he resigned from Mercury and became Leppard's co-manager, partnered with Peter Mensch. In September that same year, the EP was re-released on the Vertigo label.

'To their credit, Def Leppard's sense of self-importance and sheer balls made all the difference, as fans instantly perceived them as true professionals solely based on the fact that they had put out a record', Brazilian NWOBHM critic Eduardo Rivadavia later wrote.

Retrospectively, *Sputnikmusic* published the following: 'Considering this EP was originally recorded cheaply and released almost 30 years ago, it should come as no surprise that the production values are rather threadbare. It is indeed a shame, as all three songs contained on it include something interesting sonically. In a sense, variety is actually the EP's main strength, with none of the tracks sounding too similar to any other and any determination of a highlight track depending upon the taste of individual listeners.'

Cover Art

Alongside the changing of the spelling of their name, the band concocted a logo – a variation on the famous RCA Victor puppy, swapped out for a leopard next to an old-school phonograph. In addition, sketches of the band members were added. Dave Jeffrey was the artist.

'Ride Into The Sun' (Elliott/Savage)

Leppard's first shout-out to the world was competent enough, but not particularly memorable. Its central progression is repetitive but spirited, focused more on establishing a muscular tone than on musicality. Elliott's vocals both recall Ozzy Osborne and exceed his range, and his harmonies are impressive. Steve Clark and Pete Willis play with an energy and precision that would become Leppard trademarks. The solo is Willis's.

'It was the first song that Sav and I ever wrote together', Elliott told *Rolling Stone*. 'We had the whole thing done in about an hour. That naiveté can really drive you. And we weren't stupid – we learned our craft from listening to other people. We were students of [Pete] Townshend and [Ray and Dave] Davies and Plant and Page and Lennon and McCartney. We knew a good song when we heard one. And we just tried to rip off as many of 'em as we could!'

'Getcha Rocks Off' (Elliott/Willis/Clark/Savage)
This second track lurches in another direction entirely. After opening the EP with a fierce rocker, Leppard are suddenly throwing down a fast-paced boogie, channelling their US counterparts Boston, who had unleashed 'Smokin'' out of nowhere on their debut album three years earlier. Elliott steps up, giving us a very loose, playful delivery with no loss of power. Clark and Willis stretch out a little more in their guitar work, tapping into the song's upbeat feel. Steve has the solo. The song is overproduced, with too many echo effects on Elliott's voice, but that's what teenage bands do.

'The first song we ever wrote, if my memory serves me right,' Elliott said. 'It was a Pete Willis riff, borrowed from a friend of his who'd half written it. He changed it around a bit, came in and played it, and I started singing words over the top. It just developed into a kind of embryonic idea. And because it was our first, we were loath to change anything – no matter who might suggest we should stick a middle eight in or whatever! We were just a bunch of teenagers messing around, doing what we felt was right. But it did have a vibe about it that was above and beyond what everyone else seemed to be doing. I think there was a good reason we got the deal that hundreds of other bands couldn't seem to get at the time.'

'The Overture' (Elliott/Willis/Clark/Savage)
If 'Getcha Rocks Off' had been a sudden hairpin turn, the side-two track 'The Overture' – at 7:46, longer than the other two tracks combined (2:52 and 3:39 respectively) – is a full-blown off-the-road detour. A progressive epic work in the tradition of Rush, it features a broad surge of guitar nuance, with a clean finger-picked opening floating in atmospheric synthesiser effects, followed by bright, Thin Lizzy-style duo leadwork and out-of-the-blue American Southern rock tinges in some of the solo breaks.

Elliott's harmonies in the airy verses are perfectly executed, and we really hear Savage's bass for the first time. There are many solos, and times when Clark and Willis are in harmony lead, but Clark has the ball on the first, second, fourth and fifth solos, with Willis taking the third.

"The Overture' was very wordy, with lots of imagery', Elliott recalled in *Def Leppard: The Early Years 79-81*. 'I was putting lyrics to the mood of the music.' He elaborated further in *Definitely*: 'It had all sorts of stuff in it, acoustic bits, fast bits, quiet bits, dual guitar harmonies, a bit of Rush, a bit of Bowie. It was eight minutes long and all over the shop.'

On Through The Night (1980)

Personnel:
Joe Elliott: lead and backing vocals
Rick Savage: bass, vocals
Steve Clark: lead and rhythm guitars, vocals
Rick Allen: drums, vocals
Pete Willis: lead and rhythm guitars, vocals
Chris M. Hughes: synthesiser
Dave Cousins: spoken vocals
Recorded at Startling Studios in December 1979
Producer: Col. Tom Allom
Engineers: Louis 'Snook' Austin, Dick Plant
Released 14 March 1980
Label: Vertigo Records
Certification: Platinum (US)
Chart activity: UK Albums: 15, US *Billboard* 200: 51
Running time: 43:47

A band's first album presents unique challenges. Even after some experience cutting demos (or, as in Leppard's case, doing an EP), it's an adjustment to settle into the studio environment for days, even weeks on end. Years of success on stage in front of screaming crowds is one thing, but finding a process that works for everything – to say nothing of learning to defer to a producer – is something else entirely. It's a new kind of chemistry that can't be taken for granted, but must be patiently sought out.

So it was with the young Leppard. Having been signed by Vertigo – the label of their heroes, Thin Lizzy – they were sent to Startling Studios in Berkshire, into the arms of veteran rock producer Col. Tom Allom. Allom's hard rock credentials were unassailable. He'd been the architect of Black Sabbath's launch, helming both their debut album and its marvellous successor, *Paranoid*; he had just wrapped Judas Priest's first live disc, *Unleashed In The East*. Leppard had nothing to fear.

Good to know, but it also added to their intimidation. That was nothing, however, compared to the locale of Startling Studios: it was, in fact, Tittenhurst, John Lennon's former estate, where the Beatles legend had recorded *Imagine*. 'It was insane', Joe recalled. 'I'd grown up in a terraced house in Sheffield, and suddenly I was in the place where Lennon was filmed singing 'Imagine' with Yoko in the white room. We were in fucking Downton Abbey! We were just soaking up that whole Beatles vibe. And I drew the long straw and got Lennon's bedroom.'

It was a three-week residency, though the work itself was efficient and, at times, brisk. The band rapidly homed in on the studio chemistry that would only get sharper and more potent over time. And, as is often the case with debut album recording, they had plenty of material ready to go, refined from dozens of nights on stage. 'Getcha Rocks Off' and 'The Overture' would jump over from the EP (with shorter names); their signature anthems 'Rock Brigade' and 'Hello America' were givens, as was Steve's 'Wasted'. Their power ballad 'Sorrow Is A Woman' would be the first of an obligatory many. Two tracks – 'It Could Be You' and 'It Don't Matter' – were written and recorded on the spot, owing possibly to the inspiring surroundings.

'We got most of the backing tracks done in that one day,' Joe recalled. 'Nine songs. It was easy. Basically, it was just our live set, without the vocals.' Finishing the songs off, 'We spent too much time on the overdubs,' he said in *Definitely*, 'and as a result, the album ended up a bit too smooth. It also left me with way too little time for the vocals. I had to blast through the whole record in four days, three songs a day. For an unschooled but very enthusiastic singer, it was hard.'

One of the biggest innovations was the recording of Rick's drums on the ominous 'When The Walls Came Tumblin' Down', which were laid down in the chapel on the estate grounds. The idea was to catch the echo off the chapel walls. Another more quirky innovation was the use of a kettle stolen from the kitchen in place of a cowbell on 'It Don't Matter'. They managed to destroy the thing, and when the cook arrived the next day and saw it, she tore them a new one.

And if you're going to spend three weeks at John Lennon's old estate, the temptation to simply have fun would be irresistible. 'I took this motorcycle with me', Rick Allen reported in the liner notes of *The Early Years*. 'Steve and I would ride all around the gardens, really tearing it up. I also remember drinking copious amounts of alcohol and thinking, 'Wow, this is what being in a band is all about!"

'If I have one regret, it's that we should have recorded that album in a week and not three', he went on. 'I think we overdid it. The essence of those songs – the energy they had when we played them live – was a bit lacking. It wasn't the perfect album. I do hear naiveté. But I think that's part of its charm.'

Joe was happier with it. 'I remember being very happy with that record at the time,' he wrote. 'And I look back on it now with an enormous amount of affection.'

Future bandmates Phil Collen and Vivian Campbell, who would one day replace Pete Willis and Steve Clark, respectively, remembered hearing *On Through The Night* for the first time: 'I thought *On Through The Night* was great', recalled Phil. 'It was very different to all the other New Wave of British Heavy Metal stuff. Good melodies, lots of harmonies – it was very cool.'

'There was so much exuberance in that album', Viv said. 'But more than anything else, I could hear the deep ambition in the band.'

Based on this debut work, Canadian critic Martin Popoff declared Leppard 'one of the most polished and savvy of the NWOBHM ... a welcome breath of fresh air ... [recalling] acts like Thin Lizzy, UFO, even Queen and Mott the Hoople.'

Rolling Stone's David Fricke, who would become one of the band's perennial cheerleaders, wrote that the album 'shows they not only respect their elders, they've taken cues from their New Wave peers, too ... guitarists Pete Willis and Steve Clark shoot from the hip, packing their licks into tight, three-minute pop arrangements ... [Elliott] wails wonderfully in a resonating tenor, fortified by backup harmonies, and Tom Allom's battering-ram production ... displays a wisdom beyond their years, awfully impressive for a band making its vinyl debut.'

Creem was quick to praise the band's spirit, above and beyond their technical prowess: '...amplified zeal and spirited bravura ... this band frequently transcends the mundane through sheer musical energy and playing ability.'

Steve Huey, retrospectively writing for *Allmusic,* said that the album 'established the band as one of the leading lights of the New Wave of British Heavy Metal ... it may lack the detailed production and more pop-oriented songwriting of later efforts, [but] some Leppard fans prefer this sound.'

The band were fortunate enough to tour in support of the album, not only in their native UK, but across the ocean in the US. They warmed up for that tour by playing small clubs in January and February, then started a proper UK tour in April – after which they crossed the ocean to play two and a half months in the US.

Before heading across the ocean, however, they paid a nostalgic visit to a beloved hometown venue – Sheffield City Hall, their old home turf, where they'd first seen most of their most beloved rock heroes. Recalling that sold-out 10 April show, Joe said in the liner notes of the *Def Leppard: The Early Years* box set, 'It was only nine years after the 12-year-old me saw Marc Bolan on that stage', remembered Joe. 'I'd seen all these amazing shows there – Hunter-Ronson, Lynyrd Skynyrd, Elton John, Black Sabbath, with Van Halen opening. And now, that stage was ours. Being a headline act was what we wanted, and what we believed – naively, arrogantly, youthfully – that we deserved to be.'

'If you peer through the curtain of uncertainty that my voice was in those days, you hear the beginnings of a very good band', he continued. 'That was based on the foundation of an insane rhythm section, which Sav and Rick were, and the spread of colour that those guitarists had. As the guy who stood between Pete and Steve – literally, in the middle – I knew how good they were when they got it right. They played off each other, like opposites ... they were instinctive. It was really exciting, and when it clicked, it was unique.'

Savage agreed. 'It's easy to forget how good Pete and Steve were,' he said, 'because we were young and we've gone on to so many more levels since then. But they really were great together, full of ideas, and so tight. The band were smoking.'

'According to Artery, Leppard are 'positively the worst group ever to have graced this city with their presence", reported the *Sheffield Star.* 'That view, which was reported in an alternative publication, shows a certain bias towards bands that have been electronically tested. Def Leppard are more your Thin Lizzy. But, dominantly, they're original material, heavy rock with more than just a touch of melody.'

Off they went to America, returning home in time for the Reading Rock Festival, headlined by Whitesnake. They were not exactly hailed as conquering heroes. Reading is a town about 40 miles southwest of London, and the festival took place at Little John's Farm on Richfield Avenue (and still does, to this day). It has played in parallel with the better-known Leeds Festival, but, in fact, Reading is the longest-lived; it had begun as the National Jazz Federation Festival, which began diverting into R&B in 1963 (triggering appearances by The Rolling Stones and Long John Baldry), migrating to Reading and shifting to rock in 1971.

It was a prestigious opportunity for the young Leppard, but ill-timed. They took the stage for a 12-song set on 24 August, fresh off the plane from America – a fierce but stylistically vague NWOBHM statement that was packed with rarities the audience had never heard, from 'Long Way From Home' to 'Me And My Wine' to an early draft of 'Lady Strange' (a bootleg of the show still circulates, more than four decades on).

That they had just been off in the US led to pushback in the rock press that they were sell-outs, more interested in catering to Yankee crowds than their own native kin. Rick Savage pushed back. 'We'd played just about every gig you could play in the British Isles, from Exeter Roots Club to Aberdeen University', he said in an interview quoted on the band's website. 'There was nowhere else left to play, so we went to America, where *On Through The Night* had been quite well received. That's where the problems started. People had heard the record, they realised it wasn't a straight Heavy Metal album, and they kind of thought we'd changed in some way. Maybe we had, but it certainly wasn't a conscious thing. When we went to America, everybody thought that was why the record sounded like it did, because we didn't give a shit about England.'

The album track 'Hello America' only fed the myth, though unintentionally. Savage said that, too, was innocent: 'When Joe wrote the lyrics for 'Hello America', he was literally looking at an atlas and listing the names of cities that sounded good.'

The situation wasn't helped by the fact that Ozzy Osbourne, scheduled to appear, didn't, leading to his replacement, the well-established and wildly popular Slade, playing just before Leppard. Not really an act a young band would want to try to follow, at the time. 'Slade played all their hits,' Joe Elliott recalled (in a quote from David Fricke's *Animal Instinct*). 'And we didn't have any.'

'When the first tomato and beer can hit the stage, I knew this was it', band manager Peter Mensch said, also in *Animal Instinct*. 'Def Leppard were happening in America, and they were coming back to England, where, four months before, they were doing 85% in theatres. But to come back following

Slade, combined with the fact that people thought we had sold out, that was it, we were gone.'

On the other hand, Leppard played really well, netting not only an encore ('Wasted') but a BBC airing of five of the songs they played that day in a later broadcast. 'The legend about us getting bottled off at Reading 1980 is a myth, really – we got an encore at Reading', Joe said in 2004. 'We probably had six or seven bottles of piss thrown up – and maybe a tomato – but it didn't put us off. That 'backlash' was all blown out of proportion. We're living proof that bad reviews make no difference.'

All told, Leppard played 140 shows in support of *On Through The Night* in 1980. *Circus Magazine* awarded them the year's Best New Group honours, the previous recipients of which included Foreigner, Bad Company and The Cars.

Cover Art

The art for Leppard's first album was a clever variation on Boston's 1976 debut album, the one with a spaceship shaped like a guitar. Melvin Smith's Leppard cover depicted a heavy truck in space, toting a guitar on its trailer. The image was particularly reflective of the New Wave of British Heavy Metal's working-class image.

'Rock Brigade' (Clark/Elliott/Savage)

Released as a single (with B-side 'When The Walls Came Tumbling Down') on 14 March 1980

Kicking off with one of their popular on-stage anthems, Leppard introduce themselves to the world proper with a sampling of their sonic trademarks: well-harnessed energy, a soaring lead vocal, tight harmonies and a twin-guitar attack that recalls the fierce, controlled ferocity of its British hard rock forebears.

Even so, the song is simplistic, with a conventional verse-chorus-verse-chorus-solo structure; it's the power and the sheer quality of the performances that matter. Elliott once again has his Ozzy on as he calls his peers to arms (though he could be a little bolder). Allen serves up bold to spare in his tom-heavy, galloping attack; Willis's lead solo initially careens and bends, then goes into blistering runs over a well-crafted (and surprising) modulation from Dm to A. The result is a jump-to-your-feet rocker, more about intensity than musicality.

Released as the third single from the album, it failed to chart. The version released was not the album version, but an earlier demo recorded in September at Morgan Studios in London and produced by Nick Tauber (who had produced Thin Lizzy) as part of a planned-but-abandoned four-song EP.

'Hello America' (Clark/Elliott/Savage)

Released as a single (with B-side 'Good Morning Freedom') on 8 February 1980
Charts: UK Singles: 45

Likewise a popular concert anthem, this second track is only slightly more advanced than its predecessor, yet it throws the door open even wider. Strongly melodic and invested with more passion by the entire band, it races at breakneck speed, Elliott out front with an exuberant, almost joyous delivery, backed by a sky-high chorus. Savage's bass doesn't move a lot, but it's thunderous, which it needs to be.

Clark has the solo, which zigs and zags without losing its intensity, as Willis's rhythm guitar sprints steadfastly beneath it in near-counterpoint. Chris Hughes supplies a synth part on the choruses with a racing pulse that foreshadows the 1980s pop-rock to come.

The hard stop and syncopation right after the solo are inspired arrangement touches that foreshadow the band's emerging dynamics, which would grow and mature to full fruition over the next two albums – musicality that set Leppard apart from their peers.

Oddly, the song was widely interpreted as a sign that Leppard had sold out. 'We got totally trashed for that song,' Elliott said. 'But, Christ, I'd written it while I was working in a factory. I wanted to get out of there. 'Hello America' was like me sending out a note: 'Help!'

'It's an urban myth that we buggered off for the Yankee dollar', he continued. 'Touring the States was the next logical step for us. Led Zeppelin did it. And Iron Maiden were doing it, too, but the perception was that we'd sold out. The truth is, any of those other bands from that time would have bitten our heads off to take our place.'

The song was the second single released from the album, landing at a modest number 45 on the charts. As with 'Rock Brigade', what hit the radio was an alternate take from the pre-album Tauber sessions. (Its B-side, 'Good Morning Freedom', was an Allom-produced unused track from Tittenhurst.)

'Sorrow Is A Woman' (Clark/Elliott/Savage/Willis)
In this, the band's first power ballad, we again see early signs of the Leppard to come. The power-chorded fake-out intro suddenly drops away as Elliott begins an emotive lead vocal, supported by nothing but a light, clean, finger-picked guitar and Savage's descending chromatic bassline, as Allen keeps a ticking-clock snare-rim pulse. The whole thing then lights up again with power guitar as Elliott adds an upper harmony – the kind of dynamic shift that will one day define the band.

The lead solos are of great interest here, as Clark takes the first one, playing clean, and Willis takes the second, playing gritty, reflecting the emotional layers of the lyric – a portrait of a lover whose pain has become a fortress. As Willis wraps up the more intense second solo, the music drops low again, and a third lead break emerges, this time played in harmony by the two of them. This style of lead work, typical of British hard rock bands of the era, will eventually evolve into an even more sophisticated style of back-and-forth guitar teamwork that will become yet another defining trait of the band.

'It Could Be You' (Elliott/Willis)
Composed on the spot by Elliott and Willis during the sessions to fill out the album, this track shows the band getting their punk on. The influence of punk rock in England in that place and time was one of the band's strongest, though they didn't indulge the style very overtly. It shines through here, though, in the edgy opening riff and the song's frenetic tempo.

Elliott's vocal and harmony reach higher still here, though he avoids going for the rasp more often associated with this style. Willis grabs the opportunity to shine, delivering a solo that is too fast to be melodic but lock-steps with Allen's racing pulse.

'Satellite' (Clark/Elliott/Savage/Willis)
The first song on the album to break four minutes, this track includes spacey sound effects and a vocal pitch bend from Elliott between the verses and choruses that sounds like a starship launching in a David Bowie song. All to great effect, bolstered by more thundering tom work from Allen, the sound is brilliantly crafted to reflect the subject matter – the metaphorical pursuit of the celestial.

The stepped-up chorus adds to this illusion, along with the sonic drop-off at the bridge, which comes out of nowhere – launching Willis into a chaotic, anything-goes lead with bursts of wah-wah, wrapped up by an outro by Clark.

Not quite an immortal track, but one that speaks fluent Leppard.

'When The Walls Came Tumbling Down' (Clark/Elliott/Andrew Smith)
This ominous track wants to be progressive, but structurally and tonally keeps to its place as hard rock. There are art-rock touches, however, in the spoken-word intro by Dave Cousins (of the British progressive folk-rock band Strawbs), and the fall-of-Jericho sound effects in the song's outro.

The theme is apocalypse, with references to America, Bob Dylan and 'a terrible revenge of the gods' – articulated by the song's chaotic dynamics, Elliott's plaintive vocals and Allen's echoey tom rolls. There's considerable rhythmic complexity, shifting from a punky intro riff to a meandering verse to a galloping bridge to a four-on-the-floor chorus. Clark brings it to a shattering climax with a long-delayed solo break near the end, a screeching and wailing lamentation as dark as the song's lyric.

It's the only track on the album with a co-composer outside the band – Andrew Smith, a friend of Joe Elliott's who was serving as a roadie and van driver for the band at the time.

'Wasted' (Clark/Elliott)
Released as a single (with B-side 'Hello America') on 2 November 1979
Charts: UK Singles: 61
'The song 'Wasted' came from a riff that Steve had written', Tony Kenning once claimed. 'He ran into the room without speaking, picked up his guitar

and just started playing this riff. I think he had made it up on the bus.' A suitable genesis for an undeniably working-class rocker, with elements of punk and early British metal – and an essential track to showcase Clark, its composer (Elliott provided the lyrics). The song's harsh accents, shout-out chorus and over-processed vocals underscore the barroom feel of the song, setting up Clark's solo, where his casual indifference to modality and love for the atonal are earnestly expressed in machine-gun bursts of oddly melodic phrases, punctuated by feel-it-in-your-bones long notes. All of this would become trademark Clark.

The song was the album's lead single, backed by 'Hello America' – which ironically turned out to be the second single. Both were from the Tauber sessions, not Tittenhurst. It peaked at number 61. It is the only song from *On Through The Night* to make it onto the Leppard concert stage in the 21st century, apart from a handful of live performances of 'Rock Brigade'.

'Rocks Off' (Clark/Elliott/Savage/Willis)
Dropping the word 'Getcha' from the title, the band recycles the hot-boogie second track from the EP here, a new take mixed to have a live-audience feel. Elliott's vocal is more confident; echo is used on his voice, but with greater restraint than before.

Clark is unleashed less than a minute before the song ends, again managing to milk a sense of melody out of vast bursts of high-speed triplets, an in-your-face assault that dares you to spill beer on him. The album version of the solo sounds more natural than the EP version, owing to cleaner production that reveals more detail in his playing.

The song itself is an anomaly for early Leppard, but a telling page in the band's musical evolution.

'It Don't Matter' (Clark/Elliott/Willis)
Another song written at Tittenhurst, this track doesn't sound at all thrown together; the arrangement and production are as sophisticated as anything else on the album and then some.

Opening with a riff that feels decidedly American with its Boston-esque guitar figures, the song doesn't even get to the first verse before unveiling its first innovation: the riff is in Am, but when the second guitar comes in, it lays down a parallel major A – a grinding clash that works well in this context. When the verse does arrive, the music drops back from the big, expansive chords of the intro to short, staccato punches, giving Elliott lots of space to work. The chorus repeats the chords of the intro, preserving the unlikely parallel major A, as strong ensemble vocals let loose in Am.

Then comes Willis with the solo, played over a repeat of the staccato verse chords. He dips into Clark's style on this one, a little all-over-the-place and more than a bit atonal – but generously preserves that wah-wah pedal. It's a perfect fit.

'Answer To The Master' (Clark/Elliott/Savage/Willis)
Savage and Allen really shine on this very metal-sounding track, with the former high in the mix, laying down crisp, double-time notes under the guitar riffs and throwing in out-of-the-blue R&B garnish, while Allen serves up his first drum solo – brief, intense, but not overdone.

And before the song even gets there, we've already heard a guitar-only intro played in octaves, and Elliott's lead vocal harmonised from below, rather than above. It all works together to create a track that sounds like something completely new, with musical innovations never before explored, even this deep in the album.

Clark takes the first solo on a down-modulation that, along with some dead stops underneath, keeps us firmly engaged; he's reliably melodic until he peaks with a flurry of lightning hammer-on, then hands off to Willis. The second solo is lofty, unusual for Willis, and not only very melodic but in a major key. This is both surprising and unexpectedly complementary.

The track is far enough in to be overlooked, but shouldn't be – it's one of the album's best.

'Overture' (Clark/Elliott/Savage/Willis)
Back from the EP, 'Overture' gets a sonic upgrade: same song, same arrangement, superior production.

Unusual as it is to have a progressive epic in the Leppard canon, it's worth singling out this track for close scrutiny, both for its intricate arrangement and instrumental variety:

A clean acoustic finger-picked guitar fades in on a D major chord against a white-noise sweep, patiently waiting for Elliott to ease into the first verse; it's just the two of them, with only a handful of isolated notes from Savage until the bridge arrives and Allen joins in very lightly on drums.

A second verse comes around, and Elliott's vocal is complemented by full harmony; guitar harmonics drop in, an unexpected embellishment, and after the verse, Elliott's voice (plus the harmonies) becomes a wordless, interweaving vocal tapestry.

At 2:11, Allen crashes the song into double-time with hard cymbals and rolling toms, and Savage's bass accelerates wildly as twin guitars deliver the central riff, in Thin Lizzy harmony; on the second pass, it goes full wire choir, with a third line thrown in.

Elliott returns with a new verse, this time over a new chord progression; a second verse immediately follows, then comes Clark with a short, oscillating solo that projects nerves on edge. Elliott does another verse, and the following solo is twice as long, this time climbing higher.

With an abrupt double-hit at 4:15, Allen and Savage shift the song into new territory, this time with a mad-dash twin guitar figure in Dm that stops to look around; Elliott serves up yet another stanza, but now at half-speed and with lush high harmonies.

Wah-Wah Willis takes over at 5:02, crying out sharply, then marching up the fretboard with defiance; Elliott likewise cries out, with another wordless wail wrapped in harmony; Clark takes over with a dark riff that sets up the climax to come...

...and the song jumps up to Em at 6:01 with a riff stretching three octaves, with Savage as the anchor, following the guitars; the phrase repeats, this time with staccato drum stops to give it force, and at 6:24, the final chord sustains as the drums drop away.

The original intro, with its clean acoustic D major chord, returns in cacophonic clash with the Em, a grating but emotionally effective transition, and out the song goes.

It's not exactly *Close To The Edge,* but it's broad and varied and keeps the ear engaged. And it showcases in style the sonic strengths of the band.

This version of the song sounds less Southern rock than the earlier one, and the guitars are more smoothly integrated, less muddy; the drum mix is much better, with improved separation; and Elliott's gratuitous scream before the final solo, from the first version, is absent in the second.

B-Side
'Good Morning Freedom' (Willis/Savage/Clark/Elliott)

A grungy bar song with raucous energy and no shortage of blues-rock clichés, this track is tremendous fun, but otherwise unremarkable. Elliott's vocal isn't as clear as it could be, and the first half of the solo is indistinct; there are background vocals, but they are inappropriately poppy and limp.

The great surprise of the song is a sudden dynamic shift with a minute to go, when everything but the drums drops out from under Elliott's vocal as he sings '...the rainbow's end!' and a new guitar riff appears, jumping the song up from the key of A all the way to E. It repeats, then an octave line appears above it, and Savage jumps back in.

The key reverts to A, and Elliott does a final verse, holding his last note for four measures before the song stops dead.

High 'N' Dry (1981)

Personnel:
Joe Elliott: lead and backing vocals
Rick Savage: bass, vocals
Steve Clark: lead and rhythm guitars, vocals
Rick Allen: drums, vocals
Pete Willis: lead and rhythm guitars, vocals
Recorded at Battery Studios, London, between March and June 1981
Producer: Robert John 'Mutt' Lange
Engineer: Mike Shipley
Released: 6 July 1981
Label: Vertigo Records
Certification: 2x Platinum (US)
Chart activity: UK Albums: 26, US *Billboard* 200: 38
Running time: 42:15

Enter Robert John 'Mutt' Lange into the Leppard story, a legendary rock producer who would become to Leppard as George Martin had been to The Beatles. A strong songwriter as well as a superb producer, Lange was just coming off AC/DC's *Back In Black* – which would become one of rock's most memorable (and best-selling) albums – and Foreigner's *4* as Leppard's management was setting the table for the band's sophomore album. It was, as they say, the beginning of a beautiful friendship.

'Mutt's one of the best producers in rock', Clark would later say. 'Most producers can't explain something from a musician's point of view. But Mutt is a trained musician himself. He can change an arrangement around if it's not right ... When you're working with Mutt – and a lot of guys will tell you this – you come out of the studio a better musician.'

'For the six weeks that we were together, Mutt became the sixth member of the band', Elliott said. 'He really knows how to get the best out of a band. The sound on this album is so much better than our first one that it's embarrassing.'

After waiting months for Lange to finish up with Foreigner, the band settled in for several weeks in a rehearsal hall in London, where they walked Lange through the material they'd put together. Lange warned them ahead of time not to be 'too precious' with their songs because he was likely to 'tear them apart.'

Lange was a tough but fair critic, calling for musical and lyrical changes on songs he considered promising but unfinished. This essential early step ensured that when tape began to roll in London's Battery Studios, the material would be in the best possible shape.

Validating his reputation as an artist's producer as well as a technical wizard, Lange pushed all five Leppards to their limits as musicians. 'There were times when you thought, 'Man, I can't play it any better than that",

Savage said. 'But every time we got a keeper on tape, you thought, 'I get it – it's so much better than I thought it could be.' Mutt pushes you to another level that you didn't know was in you. And when he does it for five of you, it makes the song. You think, 'Yeah, this guy really knows what he's doing.'"

'Mutt was the most wonderful person,' Allen said, 'but he made you challenge yourself. I questioned my ability as a drummer – whether I could do what he wanted me to do. And he was the same with Joe. For both of us, it was very difficult.'

'I had to find my voice,' Joe said, 'and it was Mutt who helped me to discover it on *High 'N' Dry*. I learnt so much on that record, and most of it was about simplifying things. Mutt was fantastic for me. He wanted to turn me into more of a frontman. Basically, he turned me into the shouty Joe Elliott.'

Lange also helped shape the twin-guitar dynamic that would be a long-term Leppard trademark. 'Steve was more sloppy,' Elliott said, 'but that's a good thing – the way Johnny Thunders was sloppy, and Jimmy Page was to a point. Pete was more schooled. His chops with his right hand were bang on. With Steve, it was his thought process and his writing that made him so good. He liked to play loose. If it was a little bit out, it captured a vibe. And that was what Mutt wanted to get from us – a vibe and a lot more perspiration in the performances.'

'Overall, there's a similarity to AC/DC on *High 'N' Dry*, but it's more melodic', Elliott said of this first Lange-produced Leppard disc. 'AC/DC's music is more bluesy. It's easier to read – you can tell what's coming next. With us, we were pushing our way towards what Queen did on *A Night At The Opera*. The breakdown in 'Let It Go' – 'cool woman, cool eyes...' – you'd never in a million years hear that on an AC/DC album, but you might hear it on a Queen album.'

'It was a better version of ourselves', Allen said in *Definitely*. 'I thought it sounded way better than the first record. Mutt showed us the fantastic direction we could go in.'

'When we heard the finished album, we were blown away', Elliott agreed.

High 'N' Dry went double-platinum in the States but failed to reach the top 20 back home. Neither of its singles made the US *Billboard* top 40, but the 1984 remix of 'Bringin' On The Heartbreak', released in the wake of the upcoming *Pyromania,* went to number 61 on the US *Billboard* Hot 100 after failing to chart at all the first time out.

High 'N' Dry went to number 26 in the UK and number 38 in the US. Though it doubled its predecessor's sales in the US, it sold less than the first album in the UK. Like 'Bringin' On The Heartbreak', it was re-released after *Pyromania,* and returned to the charts at number 72. Again, the band toured to promote it in both the UK and the US, this time opening for Ozzy Osbourne during the latter.

Their sophomore effort was enough to turn music journalist Geoff Barton, founder of *Kerrang!* and editor of *Sounds,* around altogether on Leppard. 'I realise now that I wrote off Def Leppard prematurely, cruelly and unnecessarily', he wrote. '*High 'N' Dry* justifies my early faith in the band. It really is a five-star-studded, senses-shattering sensation ... *High 'N' Dry* finds the Def ones back on course and heading for a position amongst the hard rock hierarchy ... Not even the most blinkered Philistine could deny that their second album really brings the hammer down.'

'While *High 'N' Dry* cannot claim to be a resounding success as an individual album, it is indeed one from a progression standpoint', declared a retrospective essay in *Sputnikmusic*. 'Def Leppard is clearly a more confident outfit here, and with help from new producer 'Mutt' Lange, they allow their compositions to include greater scope in order for the band to find their sound. While this does result in some misses, they are never too far off target and are more than made up for by the album's highlights, which have aged extremely well.'

High 'N' Dry didn't manage to win England's love on the road, either, though once again they were given a hero's welcome in the US, where they opened for Ozzy Osbourne and Blackfoot. The album's two singles, 'Let It Go' and 'Bringin' On The Heartbreak', had charted in America but not at home.

They had preceded their second US jaunt with a UK tour alongside Rainbow, a band that drew huge crowds. Their tour set included nine of *High 'N' Dry*'s ten tracks and eight from *On Through The Night* (they wisely omitted 'Hello America').

In America, they blew the doors off. 'If Blizzard of Ozz is a modern dinosaur of heavy metal, Def Leppard is a cheetah of the same field', wrote the critic for the *Boston Globe*. 'Like Iron Maiden, Def Leppard is part of AC/DC-influenced school of British heavy metal: they let it rip. Def Leppard aren't as dexterous with melody, and they make a point of not breaking new ground, but they do play screaming, tight, driven rock with the requisite crankshaft riffs. Sure, it's bone-crushing bluster, but it's not pretentious bone-crushing bluster and one must take refuge in pleasures, however qualified.'

'While the legendary Osbourne and his band headlined the show, Def Leppard made it worthwhile for the early-comers with some pulsating, loud rock 'n' roll,' according to the *Michigan Daily Journal*. 'This quintet is a story in itself because with an average age of 19, it was a leader of the heavy metal renaissance in England last year. And even though these brash and unabashed rockers do crank it up excessively, they show real promise as a live act.'

The UK press did manage to give a nod or two, despite lingering doubts. Per the *Record Mirror,* 'Modesty has never been their selling point, and its absence is one of their most endearing features. Joe Elliott struts around the stage like the archetypal rock 'n' roll icon, but his voice has matured no end and is worthy of the attention of more than the one-third capacity crowd that bothered to turn up. Similarly, both guitarists and the rhythm section hit harder, it being no coincidence that the group share the same manager and producer as AC/DC.'

And from the sceptical *Sounds,* 'Leppard's spots have undergone alterations, no doubt about it. But however hard you scrutinize the new-found versatility, the arrogant practice stage-craft or the factor which constitutes the full-stop of any worthy assessment, the music itself, you'll detect little traces of the stars 'n stripes supposed to have sprouted on the young face of the band ... Experience usually evident in only the most accomplished bands radiated from every member of the quintet ... the new era Defening style ain't really advancement since a year ago. More a total reassessment. I like it. It works.'

They played 137 shows in support of the album.

Cover Art

The cover design was by Hipgnosis, the album art team that had done the covers of Pink Floyd's *Dark Side Of The Moon*, Yes's *Going For The One* and *Tormato*, Led Zeppelin's *Houses Of The Holy*, AC/DC's *Dirty Deeds Done Dirt Cheap*, McCartney & Wings' *Venus And Mars* and *Back To The Egg*, and many others. They had also done covers for UFO, a band the Leppards deeply admired.

'Let It Go' (Willis/Clark/Elliott)

Released as a single (with B-side 'Switch 625') on 14 August 1981
Charts: US *Billboard* Mainstream Rock: 34

Mutt Lange's presence in Leppard's music is immediately apparent in the first 30 seconds of the album's first track. For a start, 'Let It Go' was one of the songs he tore up and had the band rebuild in those early rehearsal hall weeks – it had originally been 'When The Rain Falls', and he tossed out the lyrics entirely.

Sonically, it's obvious in the song's intro that there's a new sheriff in town; Clark's and Willis's guitars are crunchy and bright at the same time, perfectly engineered, and Allen's drums have never sounded better.

And Elliott has finally found his voice. The instruments all drop back for him as the verse begins, allowing him to sound low-key and mysterious – only to burst into a focused and thrilling scream in the chorus, where he sounds (not too surprisingly) like AC/DC's Brian Johnson.

But the biggest Lange effect is in the song's arrangement. Two passes of standard verse-chorus in A are broken up when the song suddenly drops into half-time, slowing down considerably for the first solo, followed by an out-of-the-blue modulation up to Dm, with a completely new rhythm riff. Then there's another shift back to half-time, with full harmony vocals, and new lines with a new melody from Elliott – and suddenly we're back in the original key for another lead solo, followed by yet another solo in yet another key – Bm. Both solos are by Clark. That's a *lot* of hopping around for an opening-track rocker. Lange has plans for this band...

'Rock Brigade', the final single from *On Through The Night*, had been a disappointing failure in America; 'Let It Go' was the next single released, making it to number 34 on the US *Billboard* Mainstream Rock chart. The single edit is 30 seconds shorter than the album track. Cuts were made in the intro and the second guitar solo.

'Another Hit And Run' (Savage/Elliott)
The follow-up track is dark and ominous, a somewhat rigid and lengthy ride on Am that opens with ringing power chords over a galloping hi-hat from Allen. There's a brief lead riff as it repeats, then it repeats again over a subdued, clean, finger-picked figure, followed by yet another pass over dirty chords doing the same figure. The whole thing borders on tedious when Elliott saves it, bursting into the first verse with a Brian Johnson yowl that conveys anger and lamentation. The lyric is, after all, an essay on betrayal, an unfortunate exercise in bad metaphor and desperation rhymes – but Elliott totally sells it with his angry, injured delivery. The whole thing rapidly improves, with a perfectly-placed harmony in the bridge, which pauses and hovers before crashing into the chorus.

And what a chorus! It's not that brilliant, not that memorable, but it's *very* Leppard, with its inviting, audience-friendly hook – the kind of anthem you shout from the floor. 'Let it rock!' comes the harmony-drenched call, over and over, with Elliott filling in between them. This is what Leppard is learning to do so very well – come up with great hooks that an audience can shout back at them. It will only get better with time.

A dead-stop occurs just as Clark waggles up the fretboard into the first half of the solo, careening anxiously as Willis fills in beneath. There's a brief break for some connecting tissue, then they switch places – and Willis lays down a more structured, intentional statement that manages to convey the same anxiety.

The trademark dynamics kick in, and the song drops back to that clean intro passage, with Elliott slipping into it, his voice subdued and resigned: 'Oh, bring it down ... you hit me when I'm down'. There's no bridge on the final pass, as the chorus kicks back in full for two passes, with Elliott really scraping the ceiling on the last one and Clark wailing alongside him, before the song abruptly slams shut.

'High 'N' Dry (Saturday Night)' (Clark/Savage/Elliott)
The album's title track opens with an intro that is everything the previous track was not: complex, ear-catching and in-your-face. The first two bars of the intro roll out no less than six different chords – more than many rock songs contain altogether. Elliott starts singing, and it's just him, the drums and those six chords for a full half-minute. Then, Sav kicks in and the song barrels into a bridge built of a new set of chords. Then the song modulates to A for the chorus; on Mutt Lange's watch, these sonic dynamics and shifting keys will become the Leppard standard.

That chorus is another anthem, a chant – 'Saturday night!' – that repeats while Elliott once again fills the spaces in between. Willis's solo is in yet another key (E major) with Clark supporting from below with lines that very nearly qualify as counterpoint – more steps toward what will become the vintage Leppard sound. Like the previous track, the song ends with a dead stop.

There's no sugar-coating the lyrics; this is a song about getting wasted and getting laid. Elliott puts it across as exactly what it is; the result is so effective that the song made the Filthy Fifteen, a list generated by the Parents Music Resource Center in the 1980s to warn parents away from music with explicit lyrics glorifying intoxication, loose sex and violence. On a more positive note, it made number 33 on VH1's 40 Greatest Metal Songs list.

'I became quite a macho character on *High 'N' Dry,* compared to the first album', Elliott told *Rolling Stone.* 'With things like 'Let It Go' and this one, I'm this kind of beer-swilling bastard. Which I really wasn't. But that was Mutt trying to push me out front, the same way Bowie tried to push Ian Hunter out front in Mott.'

'Bringin' On The Heartbreak' (Clark/Willis/Elliott)
Released as a single on 13 November 1981 (US)/22 January 1982 (UK)
Re-released as a single ('Bringin' On The Heartbreak' 1984 remix) in June 1984
This, Leppard's first true power ballad, is yet another giant step forward in the band's journey down the musical road Mutt Lange helped them find – a template not only for Leppard, but 1980s power ballads in general. It opens with potent two-guitar harmony, laying down a theme that's intense but mournful, then dissolving into a finger-picked guitar that's so clean you could eat off it. Allen and Sav back it with a steady but solemn beat. Elliott's vocal is a lamenting proclamation, sorrowful yet accusing; he bends a lot of notes, giving the emotions he's putting across an in-the-moment feel.

So it goes, until the bridge, with its 'chunka-chunka' dirty guitars, and Elliott's voice rises as he surrenders to his feelings in soaring two-part harmony. Then comes the chorus: four repetitions of the title with its sad, utterly singable melody and high harmony. Clark's lead, with its not-quite-dirty tone and meandering register, comes across as a desperate plea. Hundreds of songs will sound like this one as the decade unfolds.

'We treat every song the same – we couldn't distinguish the ugly from the beautiful,' Elliott told *Rolling Stone.* 'But Mutt, being more of a passive observer, if you like, he was the one who realised if we had a shot at radio, it was with this song. So, when we were recording the album, it was the one that got the most attention. I'd say for every hour we spent working on another song, we spent three or four on this one. And Mutt put me through the fucking mill singing the thing because he wanted me to be accepted in the same league as a Paul Rodgers or a Lou Gramm or whoever. Meanwhile, I was just a young kid who was happy enough to be Ian Hunter!'

The song was the second of the album's two singles and went nowhere the first time out; it was, however, remixed when *High 'N' Dry* was re-released in 1984, featuring synth tracks and a video that included Phil Collen, who by then had replaced Pete Willis. That version went to number 61 on the *Billboard* Hot 100, and bridged the long singles gap between the *Pyromania* and *Hysteria* albums.

(Originally titled 'A Certain Heartache', the song was initially 'jangly', 'a kind of 'Stairway To Heaven' thing', before Lange made them tear it up and start over.)

'Switch 625' (Clark)

This, Leppard's first purely instrumental track, is all Steve Clark. He wrote it in 1976 to celebrate the loss of his virginity, and the band took it up as an effective showcase of their capacity for atmospheric guitar work.

Repetitive but never boring, it actually does manage to convey sex – starting off subtly, then building and building, growing more intense, until its protracted, explosive conclusion. Lange's decision to include it, especially as a bridge between side one and side two of the album, was a spot-on intuition: it pushes the listener from the emotional chaos of the early tracks to the resolve and determination that permeate the later ones.

'I think it's the most interesting song on *High 'N' Dry* – and I'm not even on it!' Elliott said. 'It has this very strange, angular melody that came straight out of Steve Clark's brain. To cover that with my voice didn't make any sense to me. So, I fought tooth and nail with Mutt not to add lyrics to it. I said, 'It doesn't need singing!' It kind of led in from 'Heartbreak', and I said, 'This has got to be treated the same way as the extended version of 'Layla', with the piano and the slide guitar. Or the end of 'Free Bird'.' To me, this and 'Heartbreak' were just one long song that we gave two titles. And when I say Mutt and I fought, I mean we probably argued for ten or 15 minutes about it. But I won, if you like!'

'You Got Me Runnin'' (Willis/Clark/Elliott)

Not a track of great consequence, it nonetheless underscores the point that despite its easily recognisable sound, Leppard aren't a they-all-sound-the-same band. With its jumpy chord changes and instrumentally sparse verses – atypical for Leppard – the song has an understated, matter-of-fact tone, meant to convey exasperation: Elliott is singing to a woman he's both annoyed with and enamoured by. Willis's lead is particularly inventive, his groping melodic line muttering, protesting and accusing – a great musical metaphor. The result is ultimately defiant, unapologetically vulnerable, but not at all cloying, certainly a statement.

'Lady Strange' (Willis/Clark/Allen/Elliott)

Yet another superb dual-guitar line opens this track, the evidence increasing that Leppard learned their craft at the feet of Thin Lizzy, Judas Priest and Lynyrd Skynyrd. Producer Mutt Lange's sonic touches abound, with the song shifting from sparse to big and huge; the vocal harmonies saturate the chorus, with Sav in melodic lockstep with the guitars.

The song goes into full gallop as Clark rips into the solo, a frenetic howl that is alternately chaotic and well-ordered, much like the lyrics. As he wraps it up,

Elliott unleashes vocal prowess we've never heard; at the high end of his range, his emotional tone ranging from patronising to pleading, it's clear that Lange is getting notes and emotions out of him he's never managed before.

The outro brings back that great guitar harmony as Elliott scrapes the ceiling again, crying out to a woman who has him mesmerised.

'On Through The Night' (Clark/Savage/Elliott)

Oddly titled after the debut album, this track openly gallops – a rock cliché that might seem beneath a producer like Mutt Lange. But if this tune is less a mood piece than the more evocative tracks preceding it, it nonetheless advances the Leppard sound on three fronts.

Elliott pushes harder still, crafting a high-register melody that projects intensity and urgency, underscoring just how distinctive his voice is becoming under Lange's tutelage. The lyric – a defiant surge of determination and perseverance – wriggles and squirms in his delivery, which would seem overwrought if it wasn't so spot-on.

The band's increasing attention to melody in the guitar work (on which Lange insisted) is evident here. Notes gel and surge even in the seams, and Clarke's usual blaze-and-blur opens up for some great phrases in the solo, syncing up with Sav halfway through for a glorious finish.

Finally, there's the shift from the tense minor-key vibe of the verses through an almost drastic modulation into a major-key chorus that overtly changes the emotional tone of the song from trepidation to optimism. This kind of upbeat emotional shift will become, under Lange's oversight, a core feature of Leppard.

'Mirror, Mirror (Look Into My Eyes)' (Clark/Elliott)

It's possible, though not altogether certain, that this Clark-Elliott collaboration achieves lyrical subtlety: on the surface, it's about self-confrontation, assessing a messed-up life. But it could just as well be about cocaine.

The lyric is probably the most vivid and acute of any song on the album, but the music is as much a departure or more; the verse and chorus are built on the same chords, a Dm march like an unwavering heartbeat. Elliott harmonises on the chorus, which has become standard at this point, but the rhythm of the vocals has a rat-tat-tat abruptness that's new; it foreshadows the music of Night Ranger, soon to emerge across the Atlantic.

The song's only real music shift from its thumping, self-conscious feel is in the wind-up to Clark's solo, a sudden jump to the dominant, and off Clark goes, mimicking that stuttering vocal rhythm from the chorus – and harmonising with himself, just as Elliott does.

'No No No' (Savage/Willis/Elliott)

Wrapping up the album is this bat-out-of-hell track that double-times again and again through an excellent melodic riff written by Willis, which Sav matches note-for-note. It's a closing testimony to the chops Leppard have already acquired, equaling and often surpassing those of their older peers.

Elliott's lyric obsesses, once again, over a mysterious and alluring woman who is out to possess him (he'll never stop), and the point of the song is how hard he's trying to push away. On one level, his resistance may be about self-respect, but more likely, it's about avoiding jail, as the woman in question is only 17.

The song's breakneck pace is unusual both for Leppard overall and this album in particular, given its broad acoustic palette and increasingly complex arrangements. But it's still very much Leppard, and only adds to *High 'N' Dry*'s promising diversity.

B-Side
'Me & My Wine' (Savage/Clark/Elliott)
This track was the B-side of the 'Bringin' On The Heartbreak' single, a strong tune with a compelling riff at its center and an arrangement and production gloss that recalls Foreigner. It's slightly over-produced, with Elliott's voice echoing like he's in the Grand Canyon, but it's utterly listenable – if another song about getting stone-drunk is what you're after.

Pyromania (1983)

Personnel
Joe Elliott: lead and backing vocals
Rick Savage: bass, vocals
Steve Clark: lead and rhythm guitars, vocals
Rick Allen: drums, vocals
Phil Collen: lead and rhythm guitars, vocals
Pete Willis: rhythm guitars
Thomas Dolby, Tony Kaye: keyboards
Mutt Lange, Pete Overend Watts, Rocky Newton, Chris Thompson, Terry Wilson-Slesser: backing vocals
Recorded at Parkgate Studios, Sussex, and Battery Studios, London, between January and November 1982
Producer: Robert John 'Mutt' Lange
Engineer: Mike Shipley
Released: 20 January 1983
Label: Vertigo Records
Certification: 10x Diamond (US); Silver (UK)
Chart activity: US *Billboard* 200: 2, UK Albums: 18
Running time: 44:57

Leppard's rapid rise to the pinnacle of hard rock success seems, in hindsight, almost predestined; certainly, the timing of each upward step the band took seemed charmed, from their out-of-the-gate US tours to the hiring of Mutt Lange as their producer.

Lange, on his second Leppard album, knew exactly what he had at this point and was determined to make the next step a giant one. He had already coaxed from the band a powerful signature sound, with an intensity and level of craft equal to that of heavy metal bands that had been around for much longer. Now it was time for a new conquest: the radio, and, of course, the just-emerging MTV.

That Leppard were destined to become the first true hard-rock darlings of both seems obvious in hindsight, but it wasn't altogether clear what MTV would become in its first 18 months. And no heavy metal band had ever taken up permanent residence in the top 40. That Lange so clearly recognised Leppard's potential for both seems, considered in that context, downright prescient.

Reconvening at Parkgate Studios in Sussex, he put the band through the songwriting ringer again, leveraging the strengths he had discovered during *High 'N' Dry* and pushing the envelope with every song. Part of this was born of a determination to take Leppard where no heavy metal band had gone before – superstardom – but part of it came from the fact that, despite their warm reception in the US and around the world, Leppard still weren't getting traction in their home country. A quick look at the charting of *Pyromania's* singles, above, tells the story: Lange needed Leppard to stand out in a way that no band of its kind ever had. To get there, however, another step needed to be taken first.

After moving from Sussex back to Battery Studios in London, there came a day in July when Willis was recording the solo on 'Die Hard The Hunter', and, according to his bandmates, he was just too drunk to get through it. 'He was always a bit of a beast on tour, but he was normal off the road,' said Elliott. 'But then he started being weird in the studio. He would stay up until six in the morning, drinking two bottles of Jack Daniel's. By 10:30, he was supposed to be playing a guitar solo and he couldn't even see his fingers.' They had seen the problem getting worse during the *High 'N' Dry* tour. 'Pete was becoming a liability', Elliott said. 'Basically, he turned into a drunken arsehole who couldn't do his job properly.'

During that July session, Lange took Elliott aside to complain about Willis. Elliott, already pressured with finishing unfinished lyrics, realised that a pissed-off Mutt Lange was definitely not in Leppard's best interests – and the band decided on the spot to let Pete go.

Who to replace him with? They had already made a friend of Phil Collen, a guitarist who was a few years older and more experienced than the rest of them, and whom they'd asked to step in for Willis during the Ozzy tour on just a day's notice (it ended up not being necessary). Collen was a blazing-hot guitarist, a natural showman and the friendliest guy in the world. He truly completed the band. Collen rapidly replaced Willis's lead solos on the album, though the latter's rhythm parts were preserved.

Pyromania missed the top spot on the US *Billboard* 200 by just one, and racked up an astonishing six million in sales on its initial release. It generated three top 40 singles in the *Billboard* Hot 100 in the US ('Photograph', 'Rock Of Ages', 'Foolin''), two number-one hits on the *Billboard* Top Rock Tracks chart ('Photograph', 'Rock Of Ages'), with 'Foolin'' and 'Too Late For Love' scoring in that chart's top ten. And it dragged the band up the UK Albums chart to a grudging number 18, though none of the singles made it into the UK's top 40.

Rolling Stone rated it number 364 on its 500 Greatest Albums of All Time list in 2004, number 17 on its 50 Greatest Hair Metal albums list in 2015 and number 52 on its 100 Greatest Metal Albums of All Time list in 2017.

Elliott recalled this story: 'I remember meeting Phil Lynott [of Thin Lizzy, one of his heroes]. We'd delivered *Pyromania* and, with us sharing a label with [Thin] Lizzy, he'd heard it. He put his hand on my shoulder and said, 'I heard your album – it's the reason I've split the band. I can't compete with that.' *The* crappiest backhand compliment I've ever had. I wish I had been brave enough to shove him up against the wall and say, 'Well, make a better album then!' But I just said, 'Oh', and scuttled off.'

David Fricke of *Rolling Stone* was quick to pronounce the album 'more emotionally charged than most of the synthesised disco that passes for 'modern music' over the airwaves ... may not be highly original, but they mean what they play.' Over in the US, a critic for Seattle radio station KZOK said, 'Def Leppard's *Pyromania* comes on like a three-alarm blaze. This band of young rockers have become one of Seattle's favourites in the past year. We honestly had calls since last summer asking when their new album was coming out. The delay was well worth the effort.' Martin Popoff, however, was unimpressed, calling the album 'creative degeneration ... phoney.' Steve Huey of *Allmusic* called *Pyromania* '[the album] where the band's vision coalesced and gelled into something more ... driven by catchy, shiny melodic hooks instead of heavy guitar riffs ... transcendent hard rock perfection on *Pyromania* was surprisingly successful; their reach never exceeded their grasp, which makes the album an enduring (and massively influential) classic.' The album was 'filled with tight musicianship, infectious melodies and anthemic choruses,' per *Sputnikmusic*'s retrospective review, '[recommended] to pretty much anyone ... no matter what their taste in music is.'

On the road, Leppard were finally in charge. Even on the gigs when they opened for Billy Squier, they ruled the night across 186 shows in a full year of touring for *Pyromania*. Counterintuitively, they launched their assault at the Marquee Club in London on 9 February 1984 – presenting, for the first time, Phil Collen, who fit in effortlessly and proved a perfect on-stage counterpoint to Steve Clark.

Leppard were quick to fully exploit their newfound freedom, incorporating as many deliciously indulgent set drop-ins as they pleased – including Led Zeppelin's 'Rock And Roll' and 'Travelin' Band' from Creedence Clearwater Revival. Their core set included seven *Pyromania* tracks, including the hit singles 'Photograph', 'Rock Of Ages' and 'Foolin'', alongside 'Wasted', 'Rock Brigade', 'High 'N' Dry', 'Switch 625', 'Lady Strange', 'Overture' and other older tunes.

Their newfound authority was inspiring similar boldness in their growing fan base, with a sharp increase in 'incidents' at their shows. In Lexington, Kentucky, for instance, things got out of hand at the Rupp Arena venue, where 46 people were arrested for disorderly conduct – an all-time record. That city's *Herald-Leader* quoted police Sgt. John Jacobs: 'It was a mess ... we've had KISS and we've had The Who, but as far as drunks and things, this is the worst disorder we've had.'

Even so, the *Herald-Leader* had much praise for the band itself: 'Def Leppard, though its lack of pop abilities and ambitions keep it more tightly bound to its own style and audience, showed a lot more passion in performance. The heavy metal group is famous for shocking all of its hippiest critics in the late 1970s by making a new, standard-style hard-rock group take off during the heat of the punk invasion. Their set last night was all highly polished chrome and titanium, and dealt with all the standard bogies – teen love and lust and loss and frustration and so on and on. But it was earnest and unpretentious and spirited.'

'The box office reported almost as much interest in the lead-in act, Def Leppard, as in Squier', wrote the critic for the *Hartford Courant*. 'This new British band was a perfect complement to the evening's brand of clubhouse rock. If Squier was the macho loner, then Def Leppard was Our Gang with guitars. It was also a youthful group, with its band members in their early 20s. This type of kid power seemed effortless on stage. The 33-year-old Squier was equally vigorous, but did not come across as quite so lean and hungry.'

In the *Plain Dealer*: 'Def Leppard, a British band, had the kind of energy that would have left most other headliners high and dry.' And back home, *Sounds* was growing increasingly enthusiastic: 'Can Def Leppard still cut it? Judging by their almost unnerving slick performance in the hothouse atmosphere, the answer is unquestionably in the affirmative and, in the somewhat predatory fold of HM where only the fittest of rock animals can hope to survive, Def Leppard proved beyond doubt that they are the sleekest of big cats. Whilst always possessed of cocksure arrogance and a fine brand of delivery, Leppard's Stateside jaunts have given them a polish and depth which hitherto they lacked: plus, the introduction of Phil Collen to the fold has given them a sharp new dimension, both musically and visually. Def Leppard's newly acquired maturity manifests itself in the pacing of their set. Whereas once they would have been content to 'bludgeon' you into submission, they now ally muscle with melody.'

Cover Art

Once again, the stylish Leppard logo jumps off the cover, this time designed by Satori – a company run by Andie Airfix, a British designer who had done memorable covers for Sabbath and Judas Priest, and who would go on to design covers for The Who, Led Zeppelin and Paul McCartney, among others. Bernard Gudynas provided the cover art for Airfix's design, which shows a fire burning in a towering glass office building, all through a gunsight.

'Rock! Rock! (Till You Drop)' (Clark/Elliott/Lange/Savage)

That *Pyromania*'s lead-off track is a killer concert anthem should surprise no one; concert anthems had become the strongest club in Leppard's bag. What's more noteworthy is that, right up front, Mutt Lange was adding a whole new layer to the already rich and complex sonic mix of the band.

Built on the core progression of an earlier tune called 'Medicine Man' (two live takes of 'Medicine Man' can be found in *The Early Years 79-81* box set, on the *Raw: Early BBC Recordings* and *When The Walls Come Tumbling Down* discs), the song went through Lange's tear-it-up-and-rebuild-it process, emerging with far more moving parts. It begins with a grandiose intro that leads into a second, harder-driving intro, followed by a pedal-to-the-metal verse, a B-section with its own hook, a chorus that slams out the song's title as an audience sing-a-long, followed by a bridge into Collen's solo, followed by a restrained C-section, followed by another pass of the B-section – with no vocal or lead guitar – followed by another chorus.

Put another way, the song is all over the place, and yet it feels completely integrated. This new innovation – packing song arrangements with all kinds of change and variation – was by no means unprecedented, certainly not unique to Leppard; but it wasn't at all typical of a second-generation heavy metal band. Lange was once again pushing Leppard above their peers.

'Photograph' (Clark/Elliott/Lange/Savage/Willis)
Released as a single in January 1983
Charts: US *Billboard* Mainstream Rock: 1, US *Billboard* Hot 100: 12, UK Singles chart: 66

An unfinished leftover from the *High 'N' Dry* sessions, 'Photograph' is a song that falls into Elliott's favourite topical domain: unattainable women. He told *Rolling Stone* about the lyric's genesis: 'I used to live in a little basement apartment on the outskirts of London, toward Heathrow. It was a real dump – there was a hole in the wall with a poster covering it up, kind of like in *The Shawshank Redemption*. It wasn't an escape hatch, but it looked like one! And the poster that was over this hole was Marilyn Monroe. So, I said to Mutt, 'Wouldn't it be great to write a song about a woman who's the ultimate woman, but also a woman you could never have?' He said, 'What do you mean, *Never?*' And I said, 'Because she's fucking dead!" (The song's video features a Marilyn Monroe look-alike.)

Steve Clark stands out as he opens the track with a sparse but eminently recognisable stand-alone guitar figure, soon joined by a minimal beat from Allen and Elliott's jump-right-in vocal on the verse, another lonely-boy-pining wail for a woman whose picture he stares at. The song echoes an identically themed Ringo Starr hit from a decade earlier, giving 14-year-old boys yet another validation of their lust-from-afar impulses.

And in this second track, Lange again packs out the song with ear-grabbing complexities. The rest of the band join in on the second half of the verse, and then the song jumps from E to C at the bridge – again, a section of the song with its very own theme (and a cowbell!) – until Elliott charges into the chorus, where the key jumps all the way to G.

There's another pass of the whole thing – how much pining can one boy do over a picture? – and we're back in Clark's stand-alone guitar, with Collen suddenly dive-bombing in as the lead break erupts. It's glorious.

So is the song's outro, in which Collen just keeps going. He told *Songfacts:* 'With that one, I actually worked out the melodic thing and right at the end, Mutt Lange said, 'Just vibe out on the end. Play solos and licks and go around the vocal.' Because it was such a melodic, amazing, beautiful melody, it was so easy to weave in and out of Joe's vocals at the end. Then, the chorus is so melodic that it was so easy just to play all those licks. It kind of played itself.'

'Photograph' was the first single from the album and was Leppard's first monster hit: it went to number one on *Billboard*'s Top Tracks and held that spot for six weeks. It also gave Elliott the opportunity to perform the first spread-eagle leap in an MTV video, almost a year before David Lee Roth did it in the 'Jump' video. With it being rated as the 13th greatest hard rock song of all time in 2009 by VH1, it became perhaps Leppard's most famous track.

'Stagefright' (Elliott/Lange/Savage)

This track reinforces the posturing of the band as consummate crowd-pleasers by opening with fake audience noise, a conceit echoing 'Bennie And The Jets', giving Elliott the opportunity to scream 'Welcome to my showwww!!!', enticing listeners to think of Leppard not just as music but as spectacle. If 'Rock Rock' wasn't a better tune, this could easily have been the album opener.

Again, the rug gets pulled out from under the listener as the song's verse gives way to an altogether different chorus, played clean and in a radically different key. This is now Leppard's standard operating procedure.

The song was also Collen's fire baptism. Recruited spontaneously by Elliott with Willis's dismissal, he was handed a cassette of the working version of the song by Lange, who told him to come up with a solo. He came in the next day and nailed it in one take. 'Mutt comes out of the control room with a big beaming grin on his face', Elliott told *Classic Albums*. 'He says, 'This is the guy. He just nailed the quickest solo I've ever recorded for this band.' And that's the solo that's on the record.'

'Too Late For Love' (Clark/Elliott/Lange/Savage/Willis)

Released as a single in November 1983
Charts: US *Billboard* Mainstream Rock: 9, UK Singles chart: 86
'Bringin' On The Heartbreak' had been Lange's first stab at putting Leppard into swoonspace, where millions of young women would soon join the legions of young men who were already flocking to the stages of the emerging hair metal brigades; it was now obligatory. 'Too Late For Love' was *Pyromania*'s entry, and here, too, Lange mixed it up.

Lange again cribs from Elton John ('Funeral For A Friend'), preceding the song with the sound of cold wind, evoking desolation and despair, augmented with some detached cybernoise (courtesy of 1980s synth wizard Thomas Dolby). This dystopian melodrama is wildly effective, as a lonely guitar riff appears and Elliott begins his forlorn reading, an essay on the consequences of love neglected. It's a goofy, overwrought concept, but *Wow*, the lyrics just flow, their imagery vivid and bombastic: Elliott can be very convincing when he's putting across vulnerability born of dumbness, which most young teenagers can relate to. And that, combined with this song's fantastic chorus, makes it a powerful entry in the emerging Leppard canon.

That dynamite chorus phrase surfaces immediately after Elliott's first verse, before the full band have even joined in. This is an unusual and even daring move, and yet the chorus vocals – full Leppard harmony – are so gorgeous that it just works. And with his fourth lead solo in a row on the album side – a surgically-perfect melody that wails with all the agony of Elliott's vocal – Collen cements his membership in this new incarnation of the band.

The song was the final single released from the album, going to number nine on the US *Billboard* Mainstream Rock chart, making a radio-friendly power ballad obligatory for the albums to come.

'Die Hard The Hunter' (Clark/Elliott/Lange/Savage)

Helicopters, machine-gun fire and air raid sirens open the album's final side one track – again, a recycled cliché used to pitch-perfect effect by Lange – upon which a picked pattern of clean guitar notes generates a minor-key backdrop as Elliott speaks to a 'soldier boy', whom he 'welcomes home', as his bandmates back him on the chorus, framing Elliott's narrative. The song then erupts into the first of several melodic guitar riffs, powered by an intense Sav/Allen backing rhythm.

The bridge goes to a reliably off-kilter key, returning home for the chorus, which is a straightforward chant of the title. Then comes Clark, who takes over the lead solo space that Willis had left behind upon his departure. Ironically, he foregoes his usual free-spirited lead blitz in favour of a focused, disciplined lament that echoes the tortured empathy of Elliott's lyric – and, perhaps, does a subtle homage to his former bandmate, Willis, in briefly emulating his style.

And then Lange, value-adding as he seems compelled to do, gives us an impressive multi-layer collage of guitar counterpoint, beginning at 4:01, which repeats as Clark has another go.

'Foolin'' (Clark/Elliott/Lange)

Released as a single in September 1983
Charts: US *Billboard* Mainstream Rock: 9, US *Billboard* Hot 100: 28
Lange pulls another fake-out intro as side two opens with this, the song to be released as the third single. The intro is a wash of ominous atmospheric sounds, as a finger-picked acoustic guitar escorts Elliott into the first verse, a mournful pondering of a haunting woman. Sav and Allen join in on the second half, as Elliott complains yet again that he is all alone.

Eschewing both a bridge and a change of key, the song launches into what we take to be the chorus, with big harmonies asking:

Is anybody out there, anybody there?
Does anybody wonder, anybody care?

Now, this alone would be a fantastic hard rocker: the chorus is great, the guitars alternately glistening and crunching, and less than a minute into the song, Elliott is already questioning his own emotional stability. But Lange is just getting started. We suddenly arrive at a bridge (in, of course, an unrelated key), complete with a fresh hook, and plunge into 'Fuh-fuh-fuh-foolin'' – the *actual* chorus, in yet *another* key.

Collen has already compiled a healthy share of powerful solos, but he takes the lead here, too – a contorted mass of misshapen notes with only a hint of a coherent melody – reflecting perfectly Elliott's emotional mess.

It was the album's third single, hitting number nine on the US *Billboard* Mainstream Rock chart and number 28 on the US *Billboard* Hot 100.

'Rock Of Ages' (Clark/Elliott/Lange)

Released as a single in June 1983
Charts: US *Billboard* Mainstream Rock: 1, US *Billboard* Hot 100: 16, UK Singles chart: 41

If *Pyromania* has a centre, a core, it is surely this track. It surges with every attribute that the band, along with Lange, laboured to incorporate into their sound to make them truly distinctive – attributes that continue to define them, decades on.

Gunter glieben glauten globen...

As European as these words might sound, they are, in fact, nonsense – and it's Mutt Lange speaking them on the track. He actually uttered them to count the band in on the start of a take, and it stuck. Thus, he launches the second Leppard number-one single, which opens with another great riff from Clark, as Allen clanks on a cowbell behind him. Elliot joins him with a proclamation nicked from Neil Young:

I've got something to say...
It's better to burn out
Than fade away!

The track proceeds into a sparse verse with Elliott singing in a lower register about nothing much – the song is very much a sing-along anthem about how great it is to rock out, laced with imagery of things burning (and from which the album takes its title). It remains sparse through its sing-along bridge, then goes full throttle on the chorus: 'Rock of Ages! Rock of Ages! Still rollin', keep-a rollin'!', featuring the band's first big-synth chorus (again from Thomas Dolby), sparking a tone that will light the 1980s. 'It was terrific', Dolby recalled. 'I was working only with Mutt. I barely saw the band. I think I saw Joe Elliott very briefly. But I was primarily working with Mutt and Mike Shipley, the engineer. And it was a very manicured sound for a rock record. A lot of what Mutt wanted me to do was sort of double the guitars and make them creamier and thicker.'

But the chorus is the song's only unrestrained roar: Collen once again has the lead, and he handles it with great economy, backed by nothing but Allen's rock-steady snare and a monotonic bass pulse. He soars to a conclusion, throwing open the final chorus, and the lid just comes off. No wonder the song hasn't been excluded from their live set since.

It followed 'Photograph' on the radio, also going to number one in the US, but didn't crack the top 40 in the UK.

'Comin' Under Fire' (Clark/Elliott/Lange/Willis)

This one is another obsessive screed about a woman haunting Elliott – a theme that is beginning to wear thin – but the music is a fresh and welcome dose of Clark, who has stayed in the background for most of the album to make way for the newest Leppard. His solo soars, frenetic and anxious – a perfect echo of Elliott's torment.

'Action! Not Words' (Clark/Elliott/Lange)

Slide guitar? That's new. It's not enough to raise this song to the level of the others, but it's refreshing. The song opens explosively with a blast of snare alongside major-key power chords, and proceeds pretty straightforwardly, without the expansive complexities of the earlier songs. There's a chant – 'Shock me!' – keeping it in the Leppard mode, but even Clark's excellent solo jumps a conventional whole step up, rather than through a wildly careening modulation. This song stays simple – which is not necessarily a bad thing.

'Billy's Got A Gun' (Clark/Elliott/Lange/Savage/Willis)

The album, already a showcase of stunning progress in both songcraft and studiocraft, ends with a song that's nothing like the others. It's an odd song for Leppard, but certainly an interesting one.

For once, this is a song that isn't about a woman at all. The lyric tells the tale of a young man losing his mind and growing confused and violent, spiralling into an emotional abyss brought on by trauma and troubled memories. It can be viewed as something close to social commentary, a brief statement about how society's ugly side can destroy the lives of the young.

The militant march of the music suits this theme well; Allen's relentless beat feels tense and even intimidating, and the sharp edges on the guitars have an uneasy feel. There's an urgency in Elliott's voice – one of his best deliveries on the album – that heightens the disturbing feel of the song. Collen's solo is almost frantic. The break is extensive, as if dropped in as a tour of Billy's mind. Then there's a percussive break that sounds downright industrial, as the song – and the album – fade out.

Interim: 31 December 1984

'Rick Allen, drummer for the British rock group Def Leppard, lost his left arm in a car crash and was reported in critical condition today after doctors reattached the arm', read the Associated Press story. 'Police said Allen, 21, lost his arm Monday when the sports car he was driving crashed at high speed on a highway near Sheffield, in northern England. The car left the road on a curve and overturned, catapulting Allen into a field.'

Thus began a new chapter in the band's story – one that stands out as perhaps the most compelling saga of tragedy, perseverance and victory in rock history. It would have a profound impact on Allen and the band, their relationships, their identity – and, of course, the music.

It might be a bit ironic that Allen's life would be changed so completely by a car crash – a Corvette C4, one of the fruits of success he'd harvested from the *Pyromania* album and tour – given that, when he'd joined Leppard all those years ago, he hadn't even been old enough to drive.

But driving he was, that December night, with girlfriend Miriam Barendsen beside him, when he lost control on the A57 while passing another car at high speed. Thrown from the vehicle, he was soon spotted by witnesses wandering around a field in a daze, looking for his arm, which had been severed in the crash. Both were taken to a hospital, where doctors succeeded in reattaching Allen's arm, but an infection developed, and they were forced to amputate it.

'I remember the phone call from our manager Peter Mensch', Elliott later recalled. 'He said: 'Are you sitting down?' And having seen enough movies, I knew that you don't say that unless somebody has died. But when he said, 'Your drummer's had a car crash and he's lost his arm', there's no way for you to process that information. It doesn't make any sense. I just burst into tears. I thought, for Rick, not being able to play the drums again was probably worse than death – he's going to be this walking corpse that used to be a drummer.'

'The biggest shock was when I actually came around and realised what had happened', Allen said in an interview with *Rolling Stone*'s David Fricke. 'Sitting there, looking out the bloody window, looking at myself, listening to my music. That's the thing that upset me the most at first: listening to music. I had my usual supply of tapes in the hospital. But I'd hear the drums and couldn't help but think, 'Yeah, I used to be able to do that.'

'I was never aware that they tried to put the arm back on', Allen added. 'They kept me under anesthetic the whole time. I'm glad I didn't find out about it until later, though. That would have started me thinking – about drumming again, about being normal.'

The more he thought about it, the more determined he became to find a way to do it. When Collen and Clark visited him in the hospital, he said, 'Okay, guys, listen, I've been working on this thing and I'm going to play drums again. But I'm going to use my left foot to do what my left arm used to do and then I'm going to have all these little pedals, and I'll trigger off all these other sounds, and everything's going to be okay when I play...'

'Steve and I looked at each other thinking, 'This poor kid, he must be so medicated that he actually thinks he's cool with all of this and everything is going to be okay', Collen recalled in his autobiography, *Adrenalize*. 'That he's going to be a drummer again.' It was even sadder than we had imagined. He was hallucinating. He hadn't just lost his arm. He had gone mad. How could he think past the pain, much less about ever drumming again?'

'For your drummer to lose, you know, an arm like that, I mean, it's inconceivable', Elliott commented. 'What's equally inconceivable was Rick's determination to figure out a way to play drums.' Mutt Lange was utterly supportive and positive, assuring Allen, 'You can do this!'

Allen began designing a customised drum rig that would allow him to play a set of foot pedals that would replace what his left hand used to do, using digital electronics. Once the band and its management saw that he was completely serious, they gave him their full support. The rig got built, and after some rehearsal, Allen played Led Zeppelin's 'When The Levee Breaks' for his bandmates. They were blown away. He'd done it.

'The hairs on your arm just went up, you know, it was so cool!' Elliott said. 'It was a very emotional moment, you know, there was a lot of huggin' and cryin' after that. It was stage one of his big fight-back.'

'I learned so much about friendship – you know, *real* friendship, friendships that just kind of go on and on forever', Allen told *Classic Albums*. 'The whole band, really, just banding together and just being a team, and me being part of that team was incredible.'

Hysteria (1987)

Personnel
Joe Elliott: lead and backing vocals
Rick Savage: bass, vocals
Steve Clark: lead and rhythm guitars, vocals
Rick Allen: drums, vocals
Phil Collen: lead and rhythm guitars, vocals
Mutt Lange, Gary Kemp, Rocky Newton: backing vocals
Recorded at Wisseloord, Hilversum, Windmill Lane, Dublin, and Studio Des
Dames, Paris, between February 1984 and January 1987
Producer: Robert John 'Mutt' Lange
Engineer: Nigel Green
Released: 3 August 1987
Label: Phonogram
Certification: 12x Platinum (US); 2x Platinum (UK)
Chart activity: US *Billboard* 200: 1, UK Albums: 1
Running time: 62:32

Hysteria – Leppard's fourth studio album and one of the defining albums of
the 1980s – was, to borrow from Lennon biographer Albert Goldman, the
Shout Heard 'Round the World. Almost four years in the making, it was an
album born of trauma, as drummer Rick Allen suffered perhaps the cruellest
blow a musician can when he lost his left arm. The band inhabited studios in
three different countries during the recording, and the final bill for the
sessions climbed into the millions. It was well worth it, of course; no one in
the rock universe can possibly be unaware that Hysteria was by far Leppard's
greatest success, and one of the most successful albums of the 1980s.

At the end of the *Pyromania* tour, however, neither the horror of Allen's
accident nor the megalithic success of its follow-up could be anticipated.
Making it all the murkier: as the band began to look toward the next album,
it appeared Mutt Lange's days with the band were over.

So successful had *Pyromania* been that the five members of Leppard became
tax exiles, forced to begin work on the next album outside their homeland in
order to avoid having to surrender most of their earnings to the government
(they were hardly the first; countless were the British rockers forced to do the
same over the years). They landed in Dublin, of all places, moving into a rented
house where they proceeded to begin writing the new album.

'All five of us lived in this house', Elliott said. 'It was just crazy ... the
amount of alcohol consumed was just beyond belief. But the job on hand was
to write the follow-up album to *Pyromania,* and I think the reality would be
that we were a little scared. We didn't know what to do, and so we just kept
kinda putting it off. At night, we'd just do little bits and bobs and then get
drunk and pretend it was great, and listen to it the next day, and it was
awful.'

The band may have felt insecure, but their management certainly didn't. Cliff Bernstein, one of the band's two managers, told *Classic Albums:* 'We got a call in from Dublin, saying, we just wrote this great song, we just demoed it, and we said, 'Will you send it over to us?' And we heard 'Animal' – and went – 'Uh! That's it! We got it! We don't have to worry about the next album!' And other songs followed. And we just knew, hey, all they gotta do is record these songs. This is gonna be easy! All they have to do is record these great songs, and we will have a fantastic follow-up to *Pyromania* ... it was a little harder than that, actually.'

Mutt Lange had been such a powerful presence, mentoring them into creating the spectacular *Pyromania,* that there was just an assumption in the air that he'd be in the producer's chair this time, too. But no; though he generously helped them again with their songwriting, he had informed Bernstein and his partner that he wouldn't be around – he was already committed to producing The Cars' *Heartbeat City.*

Bernstein and co-manager Peter Mensch chose Jim Steinman, architect of Meatloaf's zillion-selling *Bat Out Of Hell,* as Lange's successor. The reasoning was that Lange had profoundly impacted Leppard's output as a very capable co-writer, and the band needed that value-added ability in a producer. Steinman had written Meat Loaf's 'Paradise By The Dashboard Light' and 'Two Out Of Three Ain't Bad', and even Bonnie Tyler's mega-hit, 'Total Eclipse Of The Heart', as well as Barry Manilow's 'Read 'Em And Weep'. He had A-list songwriting chops.

But therein lay the problem: though he had produced for Tyler, Manilow and even Billy Squier, he was more a songwriter than a producer, which Leppard rapidly realised when they convened at Wisseloord in the Netherlands to begin recording.

'The problem I could see from Steinman when I was there (I went over and did pictures of them all together) was that he would do a take, and if he thought the vibe was good on the take, you know, the energy was there, he'd go, 'That'll do", photographer Ross Haflin told *Classic Albums.* 'And they were too used to Mutt Lange, who would make them do something eight million times, and then he would dissect it, and then put it back together electronically, perfectly – I think they wanted to be the new Queen, they wanted that perfect vocal harmony, perfect everything – and Steinman, to his credit, just wanted to make a good rock album, and wanted to capture the moment.'

'The thing that was, I think, the icing on the cake, the last nail in the coffin lid, as far as Phil and Steve were concerned, was, one day, we were running through a song called 'Don't Shoot Shotgun',' Elliott recalled, 'and Jim came on the talkback and went, 'I think we got it there, guys' and they just looked at each other and said, 'We haven't even tuned up yet!' 'Yeah, but it sounds honest!' 'Yeah, but to a kid in Boise, Idaho, it sounds outta tune, Jim!"

Steinman was dismissed from the project at tremendous cost: the record company had to buy out his contract, ultimately upping the total cost of the album to the point that it would need to sell five million copies just to break even. That boosted the pressure considerably.

However, the time spent with Steinman had one positive outcome: it delayed the recording to the point that Lange, having wrapped up The Cars album, could come back on board. Lange had already set a very high bar during his stewardship of *Pyromania;* now, he set the bar even higher. "Why can't a rock band have seven hit singles off one album?", Elliott quoted Lange, 'Almost write a greatest hits album before they're released?' And that's exactly what we set out to do.'

The misstep of Jim Steinman, and Allen's car crash and subsequent recovery, along with the creation of his drum rig, added to the total gestation period of *Hysteria* – but the time and troubles were worth it in the end. *Hysteria* became Def Leppard's magnum opus.

Hysteria went to number one in both the US and UK, ending Def Leppard's homeland curse once and for all. It sold more than 20 million copies worldwide, 12 million in the US, and generated seven hit singles, five of them top ten, including the number-one hit 'Love Bites'. The subsequent tour lasted more than two years, during which the band did 241 concerts around the world.

Rock Hard's 'The 500 Greatest Rock & Metal Albums of All Time' ranked it at number 464. It coincidentally got the same ranking on *Rolling Stone*'s 500 Greatest Albums of All Time. It tops *Rolling Stone*'s 50 Greatest Hair Metal Albums of All Time list, and is number two on *Loudwire*'s top 30 list. It is the 51st best-selling album of all time in the US, and with 96 weeks in the US top 40, it is tied with Springsteen's *Born In The USA* for the longest chart run of the 1980s.

Kurt Loder of *Rolling Stone* was effusive in his praise of *Hysteria*. 'This album sounds terrific', he wrote. 'Every track sparkles and burns. There is no filler. That is not to say, however, that the Leppards are actually great songwriters (as opposed to consummate riff-smiths). Because here, as on *Pyromania,* producer Mutt Lange gets full credit as a co-composer. He is, in fact, the sixth Leppard – the one who takes their riffs and choruses and assembles them into spectacular tracks ... Def Leppard seem primed to burst out of the metal ghetto. The band have shed most of the genre's more irritating stylistic tics, and it can rock with the best of today's young bands, categories be damned.' *The Ringer* declared it 'the greatest hair-metal album ever made.'

And time has only burnished the album's critical reputation. 'Mutt Lange was light years ahead of everyone when he mixed this disc', wrote Anthony Kuzminski in *Antimusic.* 'It may have been the first album destined to be played on CD.'

'*Pyromania*'s slick, layered Mutt Lange production turned into a painstaking obsession with dense sonic detail on *Hysteria*,' wrote Steve Huey of *Allmusic,* 'with the result that some critics dismissed the record as a stiff, mechanised pop sell-out (perhaps due in part to Rick Allen's new, partially electronic drum kit)' But for Huey, it was 'arguably the best pop-metal ever recorded.'

'It's 62 minutes long, it cost an outrageous-at-the-time $5 million to make, it was plagued with tragedies and delays,' per *The Sonic Collective,* 'but yet it still became a masterpiece of its era.'

Given Rick Allen's situation, the band arranged a practice tour to ensure they could actually take *Hysteria* on the road and make it work. Allen had struggled manfully to master his innovative electronic kit and pull off Leppard's increasingly powerful repertoire with only three limbs – and according to everyone who observed his efforts first-hand, all he lacked was confidence.

'We didn't know if Rick would ever be able to play live with the band again,' said manager Cliff Burnstein in *Classic Albums,* 'but we thought that at least, if we moved ahead with the project, Rick would have something to do, and he could have this rehabilitation period – where maybe, just maybe, we could figure out some way, he could figure out some way that he could play with the band in the future.'

'We'd been offered the *Monsters Of Rock* tour, basically, through August 1986', Joe remembered in *Classic Albums.* 'Donington was gonna be the first one, and it bein' England, we were nervous about just literally doing a gig, without any kind of warm-up at all. So, we arranged to do five Irish shows.'

Just to play it safe, the band booked Jeff Rich of Status Quo as a backup (it was Allen's idea), but on the second show in Ireland, Rich's connecting flight was late, and he didn't get there in time. Rick Allen went on alone and played the entire show front to back without a hitch (Rich managed to arrive and take his place before the end of the set, but he was mercifully redundant). When the set was over, Rich approached Allen with hearty congratulations: 'I came off, gave him a hug', he recalled. 'I said, 'Well done, mate, you did really fantastic!', 'cause it was, it was a big thing! He didn't think he could do that.'

The *Hysteria* tour included 241 shows across more than two years, from August 1986 to October 1988. It kicked off in Holland, appropriately, where the first serious recording of the album's tracks had occurred. From there, it would circle the globe, playing to energised crowds on three continents.

Their show included every *Hysteria* track but one ('Excitable'), all of *Pyromania*'s hits, as well as a smattering of oldies – 'Brown Sugar', 'Whole Lotta Shakin' Goin' On' and an unlikely 'Good Golly Miss Molly'. For good measure, there was a telling medley packed with their childhood: 'Not Fade Away'/'My Generation'/'Radar Love'/'Come Together'/'Whole Lotta Love'.

The show also featured a marvellous innovation – an in-the-round stage set in the centre of every venue (mostly arenas), with Allen's electronic kit at its centre and the other four Leppards set at north/south/east/west, each facing some segment of the audience directly. Much was made of this in the rock press, which presented it as a 'first', but, in fact, the British prog outfit Yes had preceded it by almost a decade, using the in-the-round format on their 1979 *Tormato* tour.

The *Boston Globe* focused on Collen and Clark: 'Guitarists Phil Collen and Steve 'Steamin'' Clark were again the most blistering guitar duo this side of Angus and Malcolm Young of AC/DC. Time and again, they shot songs into the stratosphere with ear-splitting, but never foolishly showy, solos ... Leppard's singer, Joe Elliott, left no doubt where the band was coming from on such early 1980s group sing-a-longs as 'Rock! Rock! (Till You Drop)' and the euphoric 'Rock Of Ages', which included snatches of The Who's 'My Generation' and Led Zeppelin's 'Whole Lotta Love'. Newer songs, such as the primal 'Animal' and 'Gods Of War', an uncharacteristic protest song, fired the screaming crowd yet higher. With all five band members singing at times, the effect was like a celestial gospel choir with power chords.'

It wasn't just Rick Allen's victory over trauma that made the tour a triumph; Leppard themselves were returning after an unprecedented lay-off, owing to Allen's recovery and musical rehabilitation, as well as *Hysteria*'s protracted birthing. And a lot had happened in that layoff, as the *Chicago Sun-Times* pointed out: 'While the band's three-year layoff saw bands such as Bon Jovi and Mötley Crüe steal much of metal's thunder, the interval also gave Leppard's music a chance to grow and mature. Def Leppard's recent *Hysteria* album represents a major musical leap – with melodies and hooks that show a lot more craft without compromising the band's sonic assault.'

Cover Art

The cover of *Hysteria* is easily one of the most recognisable in classic rock. Once again, it's the work of Andie Airfix; this time, he did all the art himself, crafting a contorted image of a face submerged in hysteria that suggests madness, framed in harsh angles and bright colours carried over from *Pyromania*'s art.

It's an image that evoked not just madness but menace; but 'hysteria' in this context was really a faux, contrived gesture. The only real 'menace' Def Leppard ever mustered was to the poll standings of other arena rock superbands.

'Women' (Elliott/Savage/Collen/Clark/Lange)

Released as a single on 25 August 1987

Charts: US *Billboard* Mainstream Rock: 7, US *Billboard* Hot 100: 80

The album's opening track is a sonic throw-down, a dense and atmospheric collage of ominous guitar that dissolves into a layer of clean electric rhythm before dropping to a digital bass thump as Elliott launches into a bizarrely Biblical statement about the primal nature of mating. The hooks abound, as we naturally expect, as his strange recitation proceeds – and we're into a heavily-syncopated chorus that wraps contorting guitar riffs around chants about lust. Yeah, Leppard's back, big-time.

Elliott gives us a scream that launches Collen into a solo that is as melodic and soaring as anything ever heard on a Leppard track – and everything drops out again (gotta have those out-of-the-blue dynamic lurches) into a repeat of the bridge before Elliott serves up the juiciest lyrical bits ('hair, eyes, skin on skin') one more time, a capella. It's lyrical nonsense, the goofy misogyny of junior high schoolboys, but the music is lean and muscular, a powerful arc from *Pyromania* that will rapidly send the album into new territory.

Released as the first US single, it oddly tanked, peaking at number 80 on the US *Billboard* Hot 100. 'After all the success of *Pyromania* in the US, this was released as the first single from *Hysteria* – and it didn't do anything!' Elliott told *Rolling Stone*. 'But we didn't choose it. What you have to realise is that, as a British band still living in England, we had yet to see any real success in our home country. And in June or July of 1987, before *Hysteria* came out, we released 'Animal' as a single in the UK and had a number-six hit in the British top 40. And we were like, 'This is amazing!' But our management convinced us not to go with 'Animal' in America. They wanted the more hardcore 'Women' to keep our cred factor. We said, 'Are you out of your fucking minds?'And it bombed.'

Oddly, the video of this song about women, titled 'Women', contains no actual women.

'Rocket' (Elliott/Savage/Collen/Clark/Lange)
Released as a single on 30 January 1989
Charts: US *Billboard* Mainstream Rock: 5, US *Billboard* Hot 100: 12, UK Singles chart: 15
Now that Elliott has gotten some testosterone out of his system up front, we are treated to a wonderful track that breaks new ground in several ways. 'Rocket' is Leppard's homage to the rock giants of their youth, set in a space travel metaphor (complete with sound effects and some actual NASA radio chatter from the moon). It surges with the same power and discipline of the first track, and the band break out stratospheric harmonies, in keeping with the theme.

The acute listener will latch on to the song's unusual rhythm, which is not at all rock 'n' roll. That's actually Elliott's innovation, rather than Allen's or Lange's: 'Rocket' was one of the songs that was pieced together when we were actually out of Dublin and had moved to Wisseloord Studios in Holland', he told *Classic Albums*. 'I'd been to a sauna, and I'd met this girl who had a tape of a band called Burundi Black, and this was playing, and the rhythm of it just got me going, to the point where she'd be talking away, and I was like not even hearing a word. All I could hear was, 'woo-ka-too-ka, ta-ka-ta-ka, woo-ka-too-ka, ta-ka-ta-ka' ... this drum roll thing, this tom-tom roll. And I was, like, 'Whoa! This would be so cool in a song!' So, I basically borrowed the tape and made a loop of the only bit I could find that didn't have, like, chanting over the top and recorded it on my little Fostex, and came up with a few chords over the top – which basically became the chorus.

'It was just like, okay ... let's just take loads of references ... for our generation of kids to go, 'How many song titles can you get in one song?' ... It was supposed to be, lyrically, again, nothing more serious than just a journey through the youth of somebody that was our age.' The references to their journey of youth include:

'Satellite Of Love' (Lou Reed)
'Jack Flash' (The Rolling Stones)
'Rocket Man', 'Bennie And The Jets' (Elton John)
Sgt. Pepper and the band (The Beatles)
Ziggy Stardust, Major Tom, 'Jean Genie' (David Bowie)
'Laser Love' (T. Rex)
Jet Black (The Stranglers)
Johnny B. (Chuck Berry)
'Killer Queen' (Queen)
Dizzy Lizzy (Larry Williams)

'Rocket' was the album's last single, released almost 18 months after the album itself. It went to number 12 on the US *Billboard* Hot 100 and number 15 on the UK Singles chart.

'Animal' (Elliott/Savage/Collen/Clark/Lange)
Released as a single on 20 July 1987
Charts: US *Billboard* Mainstream Rock: 5, US *Billboard* Hot 100: 19, UK Singles chart: 6
While 'Women' had been the lead-off single in the US, 'Animal' was first up in the UK – a much better choice. The song is seductively friendly and goes full Leppard into radical key changes and brief excursions, which the first two tracks didn't.

Leppard loves its minor-key drama, but this song – one of the most popular singles in the band's canon – is just plain *happy;* it's an unfettered celebration of how great it is to feel horny, and that celebration is all in bright major keys. Never has lascivious shallowness sounded so upbeat and chirpy.

The song starts off strong and loud in a bright Bb key with a power chord and a Collen riff, then pulls back in for Elliott's 'We are the hungry ones' proclamation before jumping up to an abrupt C chord for a big bridge with harmonies, rolling into the chorus in G – 'And I want! And I need! And I lust! Animal!' – made audience-chantable.

The solo is Collen's, over yet another new set of chords in yet another new key – an unlikely Dm, by way of the opening Bb. It is dependably melodic and positive, with a delighted screech at the end. The track concludes with a wink-wink chuckle from Elliott.

It was, by far, the *Hysteria* track that took the longest to write and record, stretching across more than three years – from those Dublin brainstorming sessions, pushed through the Mutt Lange Make-It-Better machine, to the final product – Leppard's first top ten hit in their own country (the single went to number six on the UK Singles chart). It made number five on the US *Billboard* Mainstream Rock chart and number 19 on the US *Billboard* Hot 100.

'Love Bites' (Elliott/Savage/Collen/Clark/Lange)
Released as a single in July 1988
Charts: US *Billboard* Mainstream Rock: 3, US *Billboard* Hot 100: 1, UK Singles chart: 11, US *Cashbox* Top 100: 1
The latest in a genre-busting string of metal ballads that began with 'Bringin' On The Heartbreak' and continued with 'Too Late For Love', this track not only enhanced their craft, but also their wallets and chart standing: it was their first number-one single.

'It was just a standard rock ballad, but it had something else going for it', Phil Collen told *Songfacts,* greatly underselling it. 'Lyrically, it kind of painted a picture, and in a song, you always want to do that, paint a picture. 'On a dark desert highway', the first line of 'Hotel California', great song, it just paints an image for you straight off the bat, and that's the sign of a really good song. It takes you right there. 'Love Bites' did that as well.' He's right in saying this: the song is an aural portrait of a man confronting a woman after the love is gone. It's as masterful a sound picture as the band ever made.

Built on a country-ish idea that Lange brought in, the song optimises the band's now-mature textured backing tracks, its complex dynamics and structural quirks, and (of course) leverages their soaring harmonies (most of which are Lange).

The opening features a bit of digital voice, which tints the song with the futuristic brush of the album's cover art, over eerie synth padding (the only *Hysteria* track to include keyboards) and a clean guitar intro, with Allen laying down a mournful kick-drum plod. Elliott musters his most bitter, sorrowful tone as he sings to yet another taunting woman, serving up questions that sit somewhere between regret and accusation. This lasts longer than you'd think they could get away with, then bursts into a more forceful bridge (in a completely different key, of course) with power chords and harmonies. The lyrics – 'I don't wanna touch you too much, baby/'cause makin' love to you might drive me crazy' – are likewise too goofy to get away with, yet somehow they pull it off.

The chorus is yet another guitar triumph, with Clark and Collen playing two completely different parts that mesh perfectly together. The harmonies are unbelievably powerful, swirling around Elliott as he spills out a tortured litany of all the terrible things love does: it bites, bleeds, brings him to his knees, lives, dies, begs and pleads.

The lead break, played by Clark over a staccato arpeggio by Collen, is clean and subdued, rather than an agonised wail – an artful choice on his part. His tone here is utterly unique, recalling, of all things, the Ozark Mountain Daredevils' 'Jackie Blue'. It's a fantastic ensemble of juxtapositions, sonically perfect and emotionally messy; a pristine painting of a disastrous encounter.

Released as a single in July, it topped the US *Billboard* Hot 100 and US *Cashbox* Top 100, hitting number three on the US *Billboard* Mainstream Rock chart and number 11 on the UK Singles chart. It remains the band's only US *Billboard* number one.

'Pour Some Sugar On Me' (Elliott/Savage/Collen/Clark/Lange)
Released as a single on 7 September 1987 and 16 April 1988)
Charts: US *Billboard* Mainstream Rock: 25, US *Billboard* Hot 100: 2, UK Singles chart: 18

The story of this song is the album's best, by far. Already months (years, really) over schedule and millions over budget, they had 11 songs in the can, and as far as their management and the record label were concerned, it was time to press the damn thing. But Mutt Lange wasn't feeling it. This sundae needed a cherry on top.

It arrived when he and Elliott were in the studio tweaking the vocals on another track, and Lange left the room for a few minutes. Elliott picked up an acoustic guitar that was lying around and started noodling out a tune he'd had in the back of his head – a countrified version of 'Pour Some Sugar On Me', just the chorus, which was all he had. (Elliott has credited The Archies' 'Sugar Sugar', a radio hit from his boyhood, as inspiration.)

'He walked in behind me and was staring at me', he told *Rolling Stone*. 'He said, 'What the hell is that?' I honestly think, to this day, he probably thought I was playing some old Kinks song or something. I played it again and he said, 'All right, new reel of tape!' And I told him, 'The guys are going to fucking go mental because they thought we were finished.' We worked on it for 12, 15 hours a day for two days. And when everybody came back, we said, 'You guys … we've kind of got another song.' And we saw the eyes start rolling. But by the time we were a minute and a half into it, they were all grinning, going, 'Fuck, yeah!'"

The track is rowdy, joyous, over-the-top bombastic – an utter contrast to songs like 'Hysteria' and 'Love Bites'. It's yet another sing-along, stadium-friendly and radio-perfect – and moves the Leppards' now-burgeoning tease great leaps forward.

The opening guitar riff is band-signature-quality. Elliott sings over Allen's explosive snare, otherwise a cappella as he lays down the verse, joined by power chords *sans* bass as the bridge approaches. The bridge modulates wildly to an unrelated key, where it stays for the 'Pour some sugar on me!' chant of the chorus. The lead break is as sparse as the intro and opening verse, just Allen's industrial rhythm and the two guitars wavering between one riff that seems to be tensely pacing back and forth, while the other pivots in the white spaces. A racy double entendre about peaches and cream steers the song into a final chorus and a foot-stomp ending.

Released in the US in April 1988, it pulled *Hysteria* out of what might have been a fatal stall; it had only sold three million copies at that point, not even enough to drag it out of the red. 'Sugar' pushed it all the way up the charts to number one, and the album sold an additional four million copies during the song's radio run alone.

'I've never sold more albums behind one single in my career than I did with 'Pour Some Sugar'', said David Leach of Mercury Records. 'It literally connected with everybody – a rock audience, a pop audience, older people, younger people – and it was a phenomenon. It sold probably four million records during the run of the single, and we shipped 450,000 records in one day, of *Hysteria,* because of the impact of 'Pour Some Sugar On Me'. That's almost going gold *in one day.*'

It went to number two on the US *Billboard* Hot 100, number 25 on the US *Billboard* Mainstream Rock chart and number 18 on the UK Singles chart. The video featured live concert footage from a show in Denver, which played endlessly on MTV and served to supercharge promotion for the tour. The 'Sugar' video is number one on MTV's Top 300 Videos of All Time list.

'Armageddon It' (Elliott/Savage/Collen/Clark/Lange)
Released as a single on 28 August 1988
Charts: US *Billboard* Mainstream Rock: 3, US *Billboard* Hot 100: 3, UK Singles chart: 20
And, once again, Leppard drops a huge tune into the top ten that radiates all that is great about their Lange-generated sound. It's got the spirited back-and-forth guitars, the luscious harmonies, thunderous rhythm, out-of-the-blue key changes and wild dynamics. It even has stupid wordplay.

The song is all adolescent sex, like so many Leppard tunes, but this one – similar to 'Sugar' before it – is as playful as can be. It opens with an inviting Collen riff in E that starts out alone, but lures in Allen and Sav before Elliott launches into his winking scold of a lover who's teasing him. The silly wordplay appears in the bridge ('Are you gettin' it?' 'Yes Armageddon It' (I'm a-gettin' it)), and we're off to the unexpected key of C for the chorus, followed by an a cappella drop-off that can't help itself, serving up the goofy bridge again.

The stand-out moments are when Elliott breaks the fourth wall, handing off a restatement of the home riff by Collen ('C'mon, Phil!!!) and later to Clark for his exuberant solo ('C'mon, Steve!!!').

Released as the album's fifth single a full year after its launch, 'Armageddon It' climbed to number three on both the US *Billboard* Hot 100 and Mainstream Rock charts, arriving at a more modest number 20 in the UK.

'Gods Of War' (Elliott/Savage/Collen/Clark/Lange)
With so many songs careening back and forth between adolescent sex and unattainable women, it might be no surprise that the band chose to shake things up a little with – well, a protest song, an anti-war anthem. As protest songs go, 'Gods Of War' is pretty weak; it says absolutely nothing that hadn't already been said to death by 1969, and it says it with no poetry whatsoever.

But whatever its failings as an anti-war theme, it is – like every other track on *Hysteria* – a killer rocker.

The song opens with a plaintive landscape of faraway sound beneath a forlorn, vaguely Scottish guitar melody, punctuated with faint sound effects lifted from the soundtrack of *Apocalypse Now* – sirens, machine guns, exploding grenades and so on. The latter is corny, of course, but also completely unnecessary. Lange is gilding the lily: this brief intro is built on long, sustained guitar notes, tweaked by Lange into a dark, devastated sigh, calling to mind the bodies on the ground after Culloden, or perhaps the shadow of Ered Wethrin after the Battle of Minas Tirith.

Then, Sav shines as he launches the song proper with a crisp and forceful bass line, joined shortly by an erratic guitar riff from Clark. Then we get a second intro riff, this one by Collen, and Elliott jumps into the verse as Sav continues his tense parade. The bridge is yet another jump off a modulated cliff with big harmonies, and this one works as well or better than most – the idea of this song is a journey through horror, into uncertainty, and this jump-around works well. No surprise that we go into a pre-chorus that we think is the chorus (in still another key), but no – after another pass of all three sections, we finally arrive at the actual chorus:

> We're fightin' for the gods of war
> But what the hell we fightin' for?
> We're fightin' with the gods of war
> But I'm a rebel

This Lennon-esque ambiguity ('Don't you know that you count me out/in') may be a bit strained, but as with 'Armageddon It', the band's most desperate grasps seem never to exceed their reach: they totally bring it home. Clark's solo is emotive and muscular. As the song fades, President Ronald Reagan can be heard threatening terrorists.

Though the song was a crowd-pleaser in concert, it did not delight critics. It annoyed Elliott that they didn't seem to give Leppard the latitude to write serious songs: 'People won't look past the ends of their noses; they think we're all Spinal Tap or Bad News', he complained to *Q* Magazine in 1988. 'Nobody will pick up the details of 'Gods Of War' like they do a Morrissey song.'

At 6:37, the song ties with 'Rocket' as the album's longest.

'Don't Shoot Shotgun' (Elliott/Savage/Collen/Clark/Lange)
Not every track on *Hysteria* adheres to the Mutt Lange playbook. This one is as straight-ahead as a rocker can get, although it does settle back into Leppard's seemingly infinite fascination with skirt-chasing. The song is about a woman who's both dangerous and unpredictable, and Elliott is warning us about her (presumably, he found out the hard way).

The song opens with a capella vocals in delicious harmony, punctuated by Allen's kick drum and finally blasted wide open with tight, controlled power chords from Collen. It's just him, Allen and Elliott heading into the first verse, with Clark and Sav joining in on the next pass. The bridge changes up the rhythm – mid-song variety that is becoming more and more common in Leppard tracks at this point – but when the chorus arrives, it is uncharacteristically just an extension of the verse. It's atypical, but it works, and so does Clark's solo. The song is a quick hit, one tidy little metaphor wrapped in enticing Leppard skin. It could easily have gone to radio (not that they were starved for singles).

'Run Riot' (Elliott/Savage/Collen/Clark/Lange)
Probably the song on *Hysteria* that most recalls Leppard's earlier days – musically, anyway – it nonetheless reaches into new lyrical territory as Elliott screeches in true AC/DC fashion about the importance of resisting society's constraints and embracing the unknown. It's a retro theme, of course, but for Leppard, it's a step forward – one that surges with the optimism and sense of adventure that defines them, behind their faux sneer and leer. The music sprints, exuberant, with metal-esque indulgences and some unintelligible guitar riffing that reminds us that Leppard march in the footsteps of truly great forebears.

'Hysteria' (Elliott/Savage/Collen/Clark/Lange)
Released as a single in November 1987
Charts: US *Billboard* Mainstream Rock: 9, US *Billboard* Hot 100: 10, UK Singles chart: 86
Now we arrive at the album's sparkling gem. Understated and easy-going, *Hysteria*'s title track is a masterful piece of work, utterly Leppard and yet not like the others: it is simpler and more standard in structure than the album's other tracks, but on the other hand, raises the bar for complex and deeply-intertwined guitar tones, riffs and melodies, which deftly convey the song's rich emotional layers.

The track was one of those conceived years earlier in Dublin, conjured up between Collen and Sav. Per the former: 'We were in Dublin and Rick Savage started playing this tune, so I immediately started singing, 'Out of touch, out of reach", he told *Songfacts*. 'That was literally the first thing that came out of my mouth. He said that was cool, and he goes, 'I got to know tonight', this whole other section. We glued it together, and we got very excited.'

'We actually went around and played it for our friends, who were clothes designers in Dublin', he continued. 'We sat down and were playing acoustic guitar, singing over the demo, and we thought that was going to be the chorus. And Mutt Lange said, 'Okay, that's a great verse, a great bridge. Now we need the chorus.' Uh, okay. So, we sat down and we kind of just goofed around. Steve had this idea, and Joe came and sang this thing, and before you knew it, the song was pretty much done.'

Sav, telling the story on *Classic Albums,* added, 'He [Collen] was playing the 'Hysteria' bridge riff, kinda like this, and I was like, 'It's funny you should say that because I've got this other idea, and it kinda goes a little bit like [the 'Hysteria' verse riff], and he went, 'Yeah, that's good!' – and out of that came 'Hysteria'.'

Those two riffs pretty much sum up the song. As said above, it is a very simple song, particularly for Leppard, and especially for a *Hysteria* track. Its complexity is in the many layers of guitar that Lange pushed them to develop. These include:

The clean verse riff, which is also the song's intro (Clark).

The long chords played above it in the intro.

A dirty guitar figure that transitions between the verses.

A variation of the verse riff with Collen playing in unison, using a layered dirty tone.

Bright, clean, ringing power chords in the bridge, with a monotone, quarter-note pulse beneath.

Collen's chorus riff – played by Clark – layered with the same quarter-pulse – played by Collen – along with the earlier transitional figure.

Bright, sustained chords to end the chorus.

Long notes faded in over the verse riff as the second verse approaches.

A beautiful chunka-chunka single-note pulse in the second verse's second half, with more long notes faded in above.

Unobtrusive, sustained high notes, dropping into the mix from above as the verse ends.

Echoey power chords, opening up the song for the lead break.

Collen's big, open, dirty-tone solo, filled with long notes and octaves, over punchy power chords by Clark.

Clark's return to the intro riff in the outro, as Collen releases a simple series of soaring, airy notes.

Glorious as all of that is on vinyl, it is, of course, impossible to play live. 'The song has 11 guitar parts', Elliott told *Kaos2000* magazine. 'What we did is make a hybrid of them into two – the ones that people could really hear and the ones that aren't important to hear live.' It is, to borrow a phrase from a critique of The Beatles' 'Dear Prudence', 'a warm bath of guitar.'

Lyrically, the song seems to be another Joe-sings-to-a-woman-he's-pining-for song, but this time his words are more earnest, his emotion deeper and more sensitive. He sounds like a grown-up, not a teenager. And yet, Collen reported that even this doesn't capture the song's true meaning: 'The song really is about finding spiritual enlightenment', he told *Songfacts.* 'Not many people know that because it sounds like just getting hysterical, but it's actually about that. It's about finding this deeper thing, whether you believe it or not.'

Released as a single in November 1987, it became its first top ten single, peaking there. It went a step higher on the US *Billboard* Mainstream Rock chart but sat at an abysmal number 86 in Britain.

The Def Leppard Report ranks it at number one on that site's ratings of *Hysteria* songs: 'Some Def Leppard songs have the ability to transport you to a different time and place the very moment you hear their opening chords; 'Hysteria' unfailingly achieves this remarkable feat.'

'Excitable' (Elliott/Savage/Collen/Clark/Lange)

It was the late 1980s, so a dance track for its own sake is no great surprise on *Hysteria*. Fortunately, it lives up to the Lange standard, opening with a playful and mildly erotic spoken collage up front, then adopting a beat that recalls Robert Palmer and Power Station.

So brilliantly processed are the rhythm guitars that they are indistinguishable from synthesisers in places, adding to the dance track feel. The song also manages to be even simpler, structurally, than its immediate predecessor, with just verse and chorus – identical in form – cinched together with unvarying chords. There's no key change in sight, and – astonishingly for this band – a mere two chords in the entire song.

How is this a Leppard song? Well, pristine production, of course, but if there's magic in the song, it's in the solo break. An instrumental drop-out, a background scream and a deep voice asking, 'Are you excitable?', create an outlandish theatrical jump to Collen's lead, which is built out of paired notes, rather than individual ones. Elliott follows with an almost whispered list of erotic enticements – leather, lace, lipstick and whatnot – in the song's only real structural departure.

The chorus explodes back into the mix once again, and then – very uncharacteristically – the song fades out slowly. Very different, very brazen and lots of fun.

'Love And Affection' (Elliott/Savage/Collen/Clark/Lange)

The album's closing track seems at first to offer nothing really new, but would be amiable and eminently listenable even so. It has the same amazing guitar work, luscious vocals and compelling presentation as all the others, though its lyric seems at first glance to abandon the maturity that is trying desperately to surface through the album's pervasive adolescence. Elliott seems to be asking for a one-night stand in a deliberate effort to fend off genuine emotions:

I don't need, don't need your heart
I don't need no understanding
I don't need no affection

Don't need your love
Don't give me love and affection

In context, however, the song radiates a deeper meaning: Elliott is approaching a woman and pleading for her sincerity. This song isn't a rehash of his animal drive; it's an essay on vulnerability. In parading his indifference to deep connection, Elliott is in fact pleading for it.

Clark and Collen bear him out: the guitars echo the open, receptive tone of 'Hysteria', rather than the zesty aggression of 'Animal'; they are welcoming, comforting, even guardedly warm. Leppard are ending *Hysteria* with a track that demonstrates their growing humanity, rather than their raucous youth.

B-Sides
'Ride Into The Sun' (Elliott/Savage/Collen/Clark)
This old track had been set aside until the band re-recorded it as a B-side for the 'Hysteria' single. It can also be found on 1993's *Retro Active,* a version that includes a piano intro by Ian Hunter.

'Tear It Down' (Clark/Collen/Elliott/Savage)
This track was the flip side of the US 'Women' single and the 'Animal' UK single. It appears later as the closing track of the *Hysteria* follow-up, *Adrenalize.*

'I Wanna Be Your Hero' (Clark/Collen/Elliott/Lange/Savage)
This track backed the US version of the 'Animal' single and the UK 'Pour Some Sugar on Me' single. It appears later on the odds-and-ends collection *Retro Active.*

'Ring Of Fire' (Clark/Collen/Elliott/Lange/Savage)
This track was the flip side of the US 'Pour Some Sugar On Me' single and the UK 'Armageddon It' single. It likewise appears on *Retro Active.*

'Billy's Got A Gun' (Elliott/Willis/Clark/Savage/Lange)
This flip side of the 'Love Bites' single was recorded live in Tilburg, Holland, in June 1987.

'Women'
This live version, recorded at McNichols Arena in Denver, CO, in February 1988, was the B-side of the US 'Rocket' single and the UK 'Let's Get Rocked' single.

Japanese Bonus Track
The Japanese edition of *Hysteria* includes a live version of 'Love And Affection', recorded in Tilburg, Holland, in June 1987.

Interim: 8 January 1991

'Steve Clark, the 30-year-old guitarist for the heavy-metal rock group Def Leppard, was found dead on Tuesday at his home here, the police said', according to the *New York Times*. 'There were no obvious injuries and there was no suspicion of foul play, Scotland Yard said. An autopsy is being conducted. He was found on the living room floor at his home on Old Church Street, in the Chelsea district, the police said. Def Leppard began in a garage in Sheffield, in northern England, and it received a record contract from Polygram in 1979. A survey in 1989 reported that the band was said to earn $28 million a year.'

The *Hysteria* tour had gone all around the world, logging 241 shows (50 more than the *Pyromania* tour) before coming to an end in October 1988. And Steve Clark, the wiry blond tornado at the centre of it all, was actually thinking of settling down with his girlfriend, American model Lorelie Shellist, and starting a family as the band took time away from each other to recover from months of touring. Clark's alcohol abuse, however, got in the way of that plan. 'We were together nearly seven years', she said. 'We had plans of getting married and having children when the *Hysteria* tour ended ... but by then, his drinking had escalated to the point of no return.'

When Elliott, Collen and Lange gathered in the studio to begin working on material for *Hysteria*'s follow-up, they got a call from manager Peter Mensch. 'Steve's in trouble', Mensch reported. 'He was found unconscious in a bar in Minneapolis, and he's been rushed to a hospital there.' (This report can be found in Collen's autobiography.) Flying out to Minneapolis, they found Clark in a rehab centre, where they were told by a doctor that Clark's blood alcohol level had reached 0.59 – 0.18, higher than the level that had killed Led Zeppelin drummer John Bonham. The band immediately staged an intervention with Clark in order to urge him to get help. He checked into a rehab facility in Tucson, Arizona, but soon checked himself out and began drinking again. Taking a six-month leave of absence from the band, he became friends with Janie Dean, a recovering heroin addict, and they became a couple.

On the night of 7 January 1991, Clark went out drinking with another friend, Daniel Van Alphen. They returned to Clark's home and watched some videos, and the following morning, Dean found Clark's body on the floor. He had died in his sleep, of respiratory failure, his body harbouring lethal levels of alcohol and morphine. Per *Adrenalized!,* Collen's autobiography, manager Cliff Bernstein called him to announce, 'Phil, I've got some bad news. Steve died in his sleep.'

'Initially, I didn't even want to be in the band after Steve passed', he wrote. 'It just didn't seem right to replace him. Steve Clark had been such an integral part of the band; he had been instrumental in creating the sound and was part of the family that we had. I mean, you wouldn't replace a brother if he died.'

'Clark was only 30 years old when he died,' wrote *Rolling Stone* editor David Fricke, 'but he had been drinking his way to oblivion for years. The guitarist had undergone treatment for alcoholism as far back as 1982 – at the same time, Willis was getting his pink slip for over-boozing. Clark had played little on *Hysteria;* Collen, who had replaced Willis in the band, did most of the guitar work. In September 1990, the other members of the band – already frustrated by two years of nonprogress on *Adrenalize* – suggested that Clark take a six-month sabbatical to get his drinking under control and his life in order. Clark died before the six months were up.

Yet it was not his death but the slow dying of his spirit that hurt the Leppards the most. The son of a Sheffield taxi driver, Clark was a 17-year-old guitar hotshot, equally adept at playing Vivaldi and Jimmy Page licks, when he first joined the band. He wrote some of the most memorable riffs in the Leppard canon, and his shyness offstage belied his dynamic guitar-hero behaviour under the lights. But by the start of the 18-month *Hysteria* tour, liquor was blurring not only Clark's vision but his ambition.'

Queen's Brian May weighed in on Clark's death in 2019 while inducting Leppard into the Rock and Roll Hall of Fame: 'They [Def Leppard] came for our Freddie Mercury tribute, which was 1992, and we've played together a bunch of times. Joe and I, in particular, have shared many precious and fun moments snatched among the madness of touring life. We have a strong bond, and he's one of my dearest pals. When Steve [Clark] died, Joe says that the first phone call he got was from me – and when the news got out of Freddie's passing, the first phone call I got was from Joe Elliott.'

'It wasn't until about three months later, when I was stuck in traffic on the 101 freeway in Los Angeles and The Rolling Stones' 'Waiting On A Friend' came on the radio', Collen wrote. 'I burst into tears. I pulled over to the side of the road and cried like a baby. I couldn't stop. That was really the moment that I began to deal with the loss of my best friend. To this day, I continue to have dreams where Steve appears and we just talk as if nothing has changed. It feels totally natural, and that's fine with me.'

'Wonderful, wonderful person,' recalled Allen, 'and certain family situations just led him into a place that was really dark. And I think a part of him didn't wanna be here. But he brought something very special to this band, something that will never really be revisited, but will always be part of the foundation of Def Leppard.'

Adrenalize (1992)

Personnel
Joe Elliott: lead and backing vocals
Rick Savage: bass, vocals
Rick Allen: drums, vocals
Phil Collen: lead and rhythm guitars, vocals
Robert 'Mutt' Lange, John Sykes: backing vocals
Phil 'Crash' Nicholas: keyboards
Pete Woodroffe: additional guitar on 'Let's Get Rocked'
Recorded at Wisseloord (Hilversum), Dublin, between 1991 and 1992
Executive producer: Robert John 'Mutt' Lange
Producers: Mike Shipley, Def Leppard
Engineers: Mike Shipley, Pete Woodroffe
Released: 30 March 1992
Label: Mercury
Certification: 3x Platinum (US); Platinum (UK)
Chart activity: US *Billboard* 200: 1, UK Albums: 1
Running time: 45:22

Steve Clark's death cast a pall over Def Leppard, one that did not and could not dissipate quickly. The band had conquered the 1980s with the one-two punch of *Pyromania* and *Hysteria,* the latter elevating not only the band but its entire genre to music's highest pinnacle. Leppard had shattered old tropes, blazed new trails and created a hybrid sound that threw open rock's gates to new audiences. Van Halen, Bon Jovi, Guns N' Roses – each owed something to Leppard. But in the face of such a terrible loss, were Leppard still Leppard?

Without Steve Clark – an essential founder and architect of the band – the question of whether or not such revolutionary energy could be sustained loomed large. Making it all the worse, Mutt Lange demurred from returning to the producer's chair (though he was happy to help with songwriting), as he had after *Pyromania.* Only this time, he meant it. No Mutt meant no amiable tyrant to horsewhip the band into writing better, playing better, arranging better and no spiritual guru to ease them through the protracted trauma of recording groundbreaking masterpieces.

Without Steve, all the guitar duties would now fall to Collen. He was more than up to the task, but it had been the synergy – the back-and-forth – of his pristine technical style versus Clark's sonic anarchy that had defined Leppard's stringwork. How could that happen now? Collen recalled working out the guitar parts of the songs on multitrack tape demos: 'I was sitting there with him when he played the original parts', he told Geoff Barton of *Classic Rock.* 'It was like playing along to a ghost.'

Mutt had been more than a producer; he'd been a mentor, and Leppard had learned much from him. It was decided that they would produce themselves this time around, with an assist from engineer Mike Shipley.

Lange had already started to help with writing the new album when Clark had died, so he would continue to exert a meaningful influence on the work. The band did most of the recording in a home studio Elliott had built in Dublin, and got on with it.

History once again repeated. Four-and-a-half years had passed between *Pyromania* and *Hysteria,* owing to a long tour of the former and endless stops and starts in the songwriting and recording of the latter. That same amount of time passed between *Hysteria* and *Adrenalyze.* History also repeated on the charts: *Adrenalize* went to number one on both sides of the pond, as *Hysteria* had, generating plenty of top 40 singles action. And in that singles action, the album delivered the UK's once-and-for-all embrace of its native sons: across them all, the *Adrenalize* singles landed an average of eight positions higher than *Hysteria's* on the UK Singles chart.

However, the 1980s were over. Hair metal, which Leppard had helped define, was over. A new sound emerging from suburban garages in the US Pacific Northwest was taking its place, and that new sound was a sneer in the face of bands like Leppard. *Adrenalize* would have the same look-and-feel of *Pyromania* and *Hysteria* (minus the genius), but it would mark the end of an era.

J.D. Considine saw *Adrenalize* for what it was, and praised it on its own terms in his Rolling Stone review: 'There are hooks of every sort on *Adrenalize,* from broad strokes like the gloriously harmonised chorus of 'Heaven Is' to ear-catching details like the little yodel Elliott slips into 'Personal Property', he wrote. '*Adrenalize* is so relentlessly catchy that it almost seems as if the band is about to abandon its heavy-metal roots for the greener fields of hard pop. That's not to say the album is any softer than its predecessors – certainly the crunchy guitars of 'Tear It Down' or 'Make Love Like A Man' are proof to the contrary – just that it's not as noisily aggressive. Consider that a sign of maturity. After all, what made *Hysteria* and *Pyromania* worth returning to wasn't their fist-pumping energy but the unabashed tunefulness the band tied to that sheer force. *Adrenalize* simply makes that connection more explicit, proving in the process that Def Leppard is one of the catchiest bands in rock. And if that doesn't make *Adrenalize* worth waiting for, I don't know what would.'

'Our overall take on *Adrenalize* is that it's a classic album of the hair metal genre', according to an essay on *Staimusic.* 'It has everything that fans of the genre love: big riffs, soaring vocals, catchy choruses and a party vibe. Def Leppard were at the top of their game when they recorded this, and it shows in every note. Although it may not be as groundbreaking as *Pyromania* or *Hysteria,* it's still a great album that deserves to be in the pantheon of metal classics.'

Elliott himself went back and forth: 'It's odd because my opinion of that album changes depending on which way the wind's blowing. I mean, sometimes I really don't like it, and then other times, I think, 'No, that's our glam rock album, we made a really cool record."

Despite the fall of hair metal and having taken another brutal blow themselves, Leppard logged a breathtaking 243 shows in support of *Adrenalize* – even more than they'd done with *Hysteria*. In Leppard's favour was the fact that Steve Clark's replacement, Vivian Campbell, was no neophyte; he'd played with Dio and Whitesnake before taking up the post he'd hold for the next three decades. His live chops lacked nothing.

By this point, Leppard's live show was leaning into greatest-hits territory, so many had they racked up after *Hysteria* – they served up generous helpings of that album, and the best of *Pyromania,* while not neglecting older tracks like 'Switch 625' and 'Bringin' On The Heartbreak'. From the new album: opening anthem 'Let's Get Rocked', 'Make Love Like A Man', 'Tear It Down', 'Tonight', the obligatory mega-ballad 'Have You Ever Needed Someone So Bad' and the Steve Clark tribute 'White Lightning'.

And they really went for broke on their choice of covers this time, folding in The Stones' 'You Can't Always Get What You Want', Bad Company's 'Can't Get Enough', Led Zeppelin's 'Over The Hills And Far Away', AC/DC's 'Back In Black', Metallica's 'Enter Sandman' and a back-handed nod to the rising tide of grunge with 'Smells Like Teen Spirit'.

Cover Art

Once again, Andie Airfix delivered the album cover – this time, a giant eyeball filled with blue lightning against a black backdrop, with the now-standard Leppard logo above. It would be his last until the decade's end.

'Let's Get Rocked' (Collen/Elliott/Lange/Savage)

Released as a single on 16 March 1992
Charts: US *Billboard* Mainstream Rock: 1, US *Billboard* Hot 100: 15, US *Cashbox* Top 100: 7, UK Singles chart: 2
Adrenalize kicks off with another anthem, and while this one preserves the best features of the preceding ones, it offers nothing really new. The guitars (all Collen) are explosive and the rhythm tense – the song feels like it's prowling.

Elliott is his usual playful self – 'Do ya wanna get rocked?' – and the song surges with the riffs, harmonies and dynamics that are now Leppard-standard. But there are no structural innovations or careening key modulations; even Collen's lead solo is straight-up rock, nothing to run out and show your friends.

There's the goofy wordplay that Leppard so love – the word 'rock', in context, is a stand-in for another four-letter word ending in 'ck' – and it manages to remind us that Leppard may be unrelentingly juvenile, but are nonetheless always great fun:

Let's get the rock outta here!
I suppose a rock's out of the question...

The text of the song is innocuous enough for a concert anthem, we suppose, but really beneath a writer of Elliott's tenure at this point in their career: it's as if he cribbed the lyrics from an imaginary 'How To Talk To Women' by David Lee Roth.

The topic is teenage disobedience – not exactly the most relevant of themes for musicians now past 30 – but the idea at the time they wrote the song was to lighten up. They'd just finished working on the Steve Clark tribute track 'White Lightning' (see below), which was a sombre experience for all, and were reaching for some fresh energy. Some of it they phoned in. The song codas out on its chorus with a half-step key change – the oldest of clichés – and then does it again in the footsteps of Barry Manilow, elevating cliché to sin.

On the other hand, there is one nugget of gold in the hills here: the verses of the song are Lange-sparse, with just Elliott singing over the rhythm by Allen and Sav. This has been done often to great effect (most notably in 'Rock Of Ages'), but this time, Collen fills the shadows with delicious, not-quite-defined guitar figures, never repeating himself, a potent form of punctuation so stylish that it rises above the song itself.

The album's premiere single, 'Let's Get Rocked', went to number one on the US *Billboard* Mainstream Rock chart, number 15 on the US *Billboard* Hot 100 and number seven on the US *Cashbox* Top 100, while climbing to number two on the UK Singles chart.

'Heaven Is' (Clark/Collen/Elliott/Lange/Savage)
Released as a single on 18 January 1993
Charts: UK Singles chart: 13
The follow-up track opens with clean, fingerpicked guitar, then shifts key wildly, from D major to B major, for a verse built on crunchy power chords. *That's* the Leppard we're used to.

The bridge, jumping up to E, uses a Boston innovation, with Collen mimicking Elliott's melody before the chorus modulates to a delightful G – unprecedented, unexpected and a real thrill to the ear. The solo break careens even more, shifting key from A to F to G and then back to B of the verse, where Collen really takes off.

Once again, Elliott is worshipping a woman who's smarter and more self-aware than he is, but the hard lean into upbeat, positive energy in the face of such dysfunction has long since become a feature, not a bug. Elliott even said that the backing vocals on the song's chorus were a deliberate homage to The Beach Boys, and it doesn't get much more upbeat and positive than that. Collen said the song had been around for some time before finally landing here, and that they raided 'Armageddon It' for some of its structure.

Released as the album's penultimate single in January 1993, it made number 13 on the UK Singles chart.

'Make Love Like A Man' (Clark/Collen/Elliott/Lange)
Released as a single on 15 June 1992
Charts: US *Billboard* Mainstream Rock: 3, US *Billboard* Hot 100: 36, UK Singles chart: 12
A third song (in a row) opining about meaningless, consequence-free sex might seem excessive even for Leppard, but this one has the virtue of being intentionally self-effacing: Elliott is *admitting* that it has become ridiculous, and this buoyant, melody-laden tune makes for an endearing apology. Elliott may have been admitting it because he simply had no choice. No one can hear a lyric like this without rolling one's eyes:

I'm the one
(I got it) I'm Mr. Fun
(You need it) I'm captain cool
(Come get it) and I've come for you
Come on
Don't call me gigolo, don't call me Casanova
Just call me on the phone and baby come on over
When you need someone, when you need someone to
Make love like a man
I'm a man, well, that's what I am, yeah

Elliott's confession to this effect is found in the liner notes of the band's collection *Vault,* where he states that the song's macho tone is frivolous and that they were trying to be funny. He later said to *Iheartradio* in April 2020 that he didn't particularly want to keep playing the song live because the lyrics 'were a nod too stupid.'

Subject matter aside, this is a well-crafted tune. Built on a sturdy, unyielding rhythm and an impudent lead vocal from Elliott, it changes up into breezy bridge harmonies that borrow shamelessly from pop, as if ABBA were sitting in. Even so, it all fits into this hard-edged track seamlessly. The track was the album's second single, hitting the radio in June 1992 and going to number three on the US *Billboard* Mainstream Rock chart and number 36 on the Hot 100. It went to number 12 on the UK Singles chart.

'Tonight' (Clark/Collen/Elliott/Lange/Savage)
Released as a single on 19 April 1993
Charts: US *Billboard* Mainstream Rock: 13, US *Billboard* Hot 100: 62, UK Singles chart: 34
'Tonight' makes it four in a row, as it is yet another song about getting laid, but this one is musically the best of the lot, a track with a haunting facade that recalls 'Too Late For Love'. Collen stretches out stylistically, opening the song with fingerpicked acoustic guitar, then providing his own chunky backing on electric, throwing down a tense rhythm guitar and tormented riff

in the chorus. Elliott serves up yet another tortured lamentation, but even he sounds renewed. There's some ambiguity in the story he's telling, some emotional complexity: the woman he's singing to seems neither intimidating nor disposable; she might even be, in his eyes, a keeper.

Leppard's harmonies are always superb, but these are standouts. Collen's lead is an emotive 1970s throwback, fraught with suspense and surging tension, and the track further manages to be different by remaining in the same key. It scarcely ever moves off its root chord. The only other track that is comparably static in the Leppard canon might be 'Excitable'; this track is more impactful, standing out as one of this album's best.

Recorded during a break in the *Hysteria* tour as a possible B-side for one of that album's singles, it was benched and then re-recorded for *Adrenalize.* 'Tonight' was the album's final single, released in April 1993, over a year after the launch of *Adrenalize.* It hit number 13 on the US *Billboard* Mainstream Rock chart and number 62 on the US *Billboard* Hot 100, with a number 34 placement on the UK Singles chart.

'White Lightning' (Collen/Elliott/Lange/Savage)
Leppard's tribute to its lost co-founder is the most substantial track on the album, not just meaningful in content but powerful in musical composition and execution. The previous tracks have been generally playful; 'White Lightning' lets us know the boys are about to get serious.

It begins as a dirge, Collen laying down a mournful melody line over a low, humming drone. Another overlaps it, then another, and when the rhythm kicks in and Elliott begins to sing, there is no bombast, no flash – just a sombre recitation as the band turn to its missing man.

It's a song that pulls no punches; it's clearly about Clark, 'White Lightning' being an early nickname for him based on his stage persona, but much of the lyric alludes to the seductive lure of addiction:

You want to ride White Lightnin'
Then sign your name
If you want to dance with the devil
You gotta play his way, play the game
You gotta taste that sweetness
Cause you can't say no
But are you ready for the nightmare
When you can't let go

'We wanted it to be about Steve, but we also wanted anybody who was listening to it and had been in a similar situation to be able to relate to it', Elliott told *Rolling Stone.* 'So, we never mention him by name. But the situations he found himself in, and the situations he put us in, are all kind of referenced, without getting overly specific.'

The core Gm riffs by Collen were the song's starting point, with Elliott deciding early on that the song they were suggesting was something that should showcase Clark. The track is neither structured nor produced with the ear-candy layering of so many Leppard artefacts; it's straightforward, focused on its message.

That said, the bridge that follows Elliott's haunted exposition of the theme hangs on a choral hook, many voices as one, that is both memorable and exuberant; it is a sad song that is also a celebration. And, of course, it's in A major, a big jump from Elliott's dark verse. This emotional shift is an emphatic salute to Clark, a mash-up of sadness and joy.

The chorus is as plaintive as it is glorious, a full harmony statement that sends Elliott's melody to the peak of his vocal register. Collen's solo break, also in that sad/joyful key of A, is frenetic and almost desperate, an asymptotic reaching for a destination beyond him; it searches and searches, casting about into familiar sonic corners with a few lurches into amodal sinkholes – 'Where's Steve?', he's asking musically.

Elliott has said that he considers it the album's most memorable track.

'Stand Up (Kick Love Into Motion)' (Clark/Collen/Elliott/Lange)
Released as a single on 4 December 1992
Charts: US *Billboard* Mainstream Rock: 1, US *Billboard* Hot 100: 34
This wonderful track is *Adrenalize*'s 'Hysteria', the mid-tempo delight that's not like the others. It was, in fact, primarily written by Collen and Clark at Wisseloord for the *Hysteria* album, but was shelved precisely because it sounded too much like that title track.

Starting off with a hanging riff that sounds like it's echoing through the Scottish Highlands, 'Stand Up' proceeds into that same mellow groove, with layered sonic pads emanating from Collen that radiate the anticipation and earnestness in Elliott's vocal – a rare and impassioned plea, not for sex, but for true connection. The track is one of those make-or-break love songs where the troubadour is putting himself on the line, pouring his heart out – and it's about time, after Leppard's decade-plus of adolescent antics. Elliott's sincere petition is downright vulnerable, and the band give it unflinching support. The rhythm is tentative, Collen's guitars are contained but restless and the chorus harmonies are jubilant. It's like Elliott is singing from beneath his love's balcony and the band are standing behind him, backing him up.

Preserving this inspiring focus, the song stays structurally conventional; there are no wild shifts and no unexpected modulations. It's a standard verse-chorus affair, with the same key retained in both sections. Then there's a middle-eight, of all things, which may be the most old-fashioned Leppard has ever gotten. Collen's solo soars, and likewise has a callback feel, evoking an age when love songs were less erotic and more about devotion. There's a sparse after-solo break in which Elliott's voice surges with determination before a final chorus takes his appeal home.

Above: Def Leppard in their Union Jack stage gear, an overt nod to their British identity, during the 1983 *Pyromania* tour.

Left: The cover of the self-produced *Def Leppard EP* (1979), with artwork by Dave Jeffery (intended as a spoof of the famous RCA gramophone logo). (*Bludgeon-Riffola*)

Right: The cover of *On Through The Night* (1980), Leppard's first full studio album, with artwork by Alan Schmidt. It was the first cover to feature Leppard's signature logo. (*Vertigo*)

Right: The cover of *High 'N' Dry* (1981), the first Mutt Lange-produced album, with conceptual art by Hipgnosis. (*Vertigo*)

Left: The cover of *Pyromania* (1983), Leppard's breakthrough album, with design by Satori and artwork by Bernard Gudynas. (*Vertigo*)

Above: An early promo shot of Rick Savage, Joe Elliott, Pete Willis, Rick Allen and Steve Clark in the 1970s. (*Chris Walter/WireImage*)

Below: Joe Elliott, Rick Savage, Pete Willis, Rick Allen and Steve Clark in 1979. (*Chris Walter/WireImage*)

Above: Def Leppard at New York's Palladium Theater on their first US tour, 8 January 1980. (*Bill O'Leary*)

Below: Joe Elliott at Parkgate Studio, East Sussex, during the *Pyromania* sessions in the summer of 1982. (*PG Brunelli*)

Left: The cover of *Hysteria* (1987), with design and artwork by Andie Airfix (Satori). (*Mercury*)

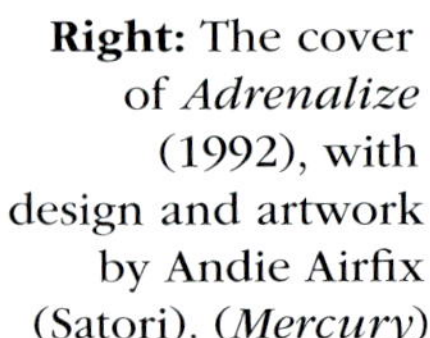

Right: The cover of *Adrenalize* (1992), with design and artwork by Andie Airfix (Satori). (*Mercury*)

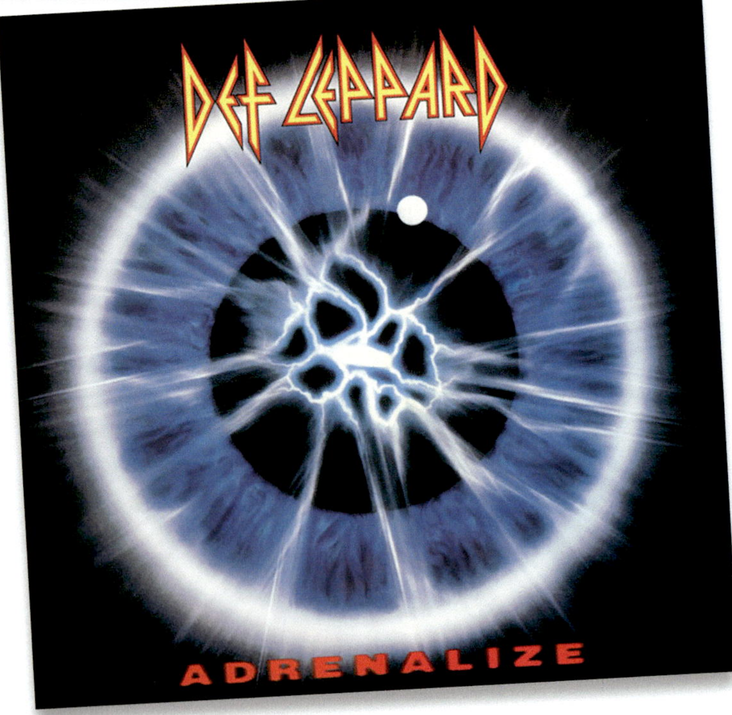

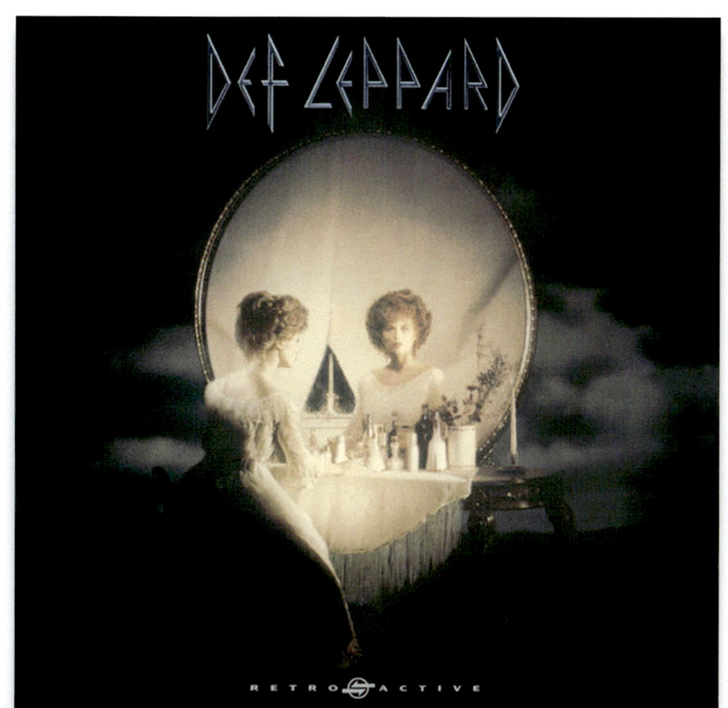

Right: The conceptual cover of *Retro Active* (1993), with artwork – inspired by Charles Allan Gilbert's *All Is Vanity* – by Nels Israelson and Hugh Syme. (*Mercury*)

Left: The cover of 1996's *Slang* – the first Leppard studio album *not* to feature their signature logo. (*Mercury*)

Left: The *Gunter-Gleiben-Glauchen-Globen* intro from the 'Rock Of Ages' music video, 1983.

Right: Rick Savage, Joe Elliott and Phil Collen in the 'Rock Of Ages' music video. (*Warner Bros.*)

Left: Joe Elliott in the 'Foolin'' music video, 1983.

Right: Rick Savage in the 'Animal' music video, 1987. The track was Leppard's first top ten single in their homeland.

Left: Rick Allen in the 'Animal' music video.

Right: Joe Elliott and Phil Collen in the band's performance of 'Rocket' on *Top Of The Pops* on 16 February 1989. It was Steve Clark's final television appearance with the band before his death the following year.

Above: Rick Allen during a show at the Hartford Civic Center on the American leg of Leppard's *Hysteria* tour, 11 October 1987. (*John Atashian/Getty Images*)

Below: Joe Elliott during the *Hysteria* tour. (*Ross Halfin*)

Above: The band (with Brian May far right) at the Freddie Mercury Tribute Concert, Wembley, London, on 20 April 1992. May joined Leppard on 'Now I'm Here'. (*Michael Putland/Getty Images*)

Below: Rick Savage, Vivian Campbell, Joe Elliott, Rick Allen and Phil Collen in a promotional photo from the *Euphoria* tour, 1999. (*Def Leppard*)

Left: The return-to-form cover of *Euphoria* (1999), with artwork by Andie Airfix. (*Mercury*)

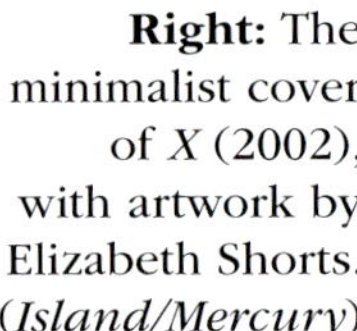

Right: The minimalist cover of *X* (2002), with artwork by Elizabeth Shorts. (*Island/Mercury*)

Right: The cover of *Yeah!* (2006), with artwork by t42design, art direction by Vartan and cover art photography by Clay Patrick McBride. (*Mercury/ Island*)

Left: The cover of *Songs From The Sparkle Lounge* (2008) was designed and created by Richard Proctor, intended to recall *Sgt. Pepper's Lonely Hearts Club Band*. (*Island/ Universal Music Enterprises/ Mercury*)

Left: The cover of the self-titled *Def Leppard* (2015) album, with another minimalist design, this one by Richard Smith Illustration. (*Mailboat/ earMUSIC*)

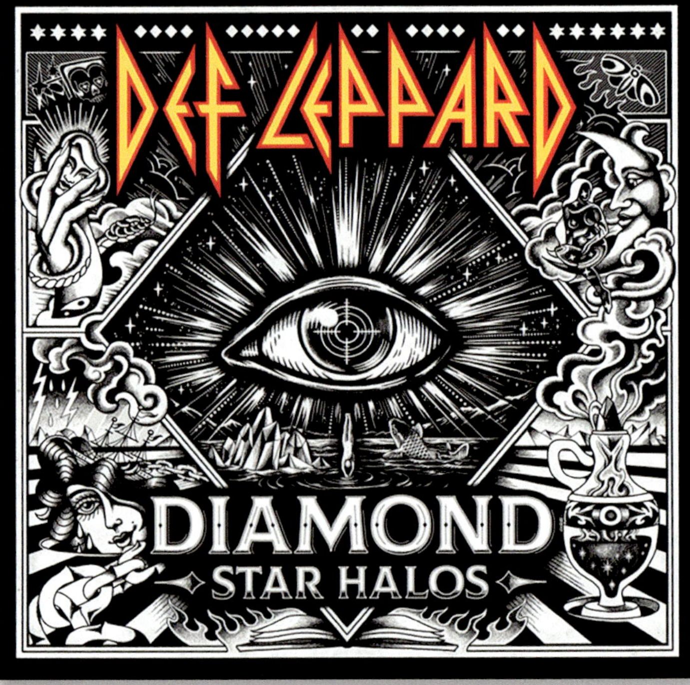

Right: The cover of *Diamond Star Halos* (2022), with artwork by Oliver and Joshua Munden, and photography by Anton Corbijn. (*Mercury*)

Above: Rick Savage, Joe Elliott and Phil Collen at the Hollywood and Highland entertainment complex in Los Angeles on 8 June 2012. (*Kevin Winter/Getty Images*)

Below: Def Leppard at the 2019 Rock and Roll Hall of Fame ceremony. Brian May (not pictured) inducted them. (*Kevin Kane/Getty Images*)

Left: The cover of the 1995 greatest-hits collection *Vault*, with design and artwork by Exquisite Corpse and photography by Cynthia Levine and Ross Halfin. (*Mercury*)

Right: The cover of *Mirror Ball – Live & More* (2011); Leppard contributed to the art direction, with Richard Proctor and Richie Burford doing the actual design and artwork. (*Mailboat*)

Left: The cover of the double-live album *Viva Hysteria!* (2013), with design and artwork by Andie Airfix (Satori). (*Frontiers*)

The album's fourth single, released in December 1992, it went to number one on the US *Billboard* Album Rock chart and number 34 on the *Billboard* Hot 100.

'Personal Property' (Collen/Elliott/Lange/Savage)
A track that would qualify as filler if the lyric wasn't so revealing, 'Personal Property' is nonetheless authentic Leppard, with a tight, punchy rhythm, bounce-around key modulations and endlessly creative guitar work. The chorus is uncharacteristically clumsy, but Collen's lead break is reliably noteworthy and exhilarating.

Another song about a woman, its theme seems at first to be possessiveness:

It's finder's keepers
Loser's gonna weep
She's personal, property
Sealed 'n' stamped
Money in the bank
She's private
For my eyes only

This begs us to address the problematic issue of woman-as-property, but there's enough going on here that it's probably simpler to just acknowledge the progress made peripherally in Leppard's messaging about relationships: monogamy rocks. Embrace it. Take the win.

'Have You Ever Needed Someone So Bad' (Collen/Elliott/Lange)
Released as a single on 31 August 1992
Charts: US *Billboard* Mainstream Rock: 7, US *Billboard* Hot 100: 12, UK Singles chart: 16
The album's obligatory power ballad is tucked away near the end of the album, and just as well: it doesn't glisten like its predecessors, or rise to their standard, though it rises pretty high among 1980s power ballads generally. Collen's opening riff is somewhat conventional, but it works well. The rest of the song is more conventional still, a generic power ballad, and even the chorus and its harmonies, catchy as they are, seem overly familiar. This track badly needed Lange's haranguing influence.

That said, Collen's solo riff and Elliott's breathless middle-eight have a tension that is spot-on, and the outro serves up layers of delicious guitar. But in the end, this song owes much to Heart's 'What About Love?', which is simply a much better song.

The song was the album's third single, released in August 1992 and scoring a number 37 placement on the US *Billboard* Mainstream Rock chart, a number 12 placement on the *Billboard* Hot 100 and a number 16 placement on the UK Singles chart.

'I Wanna Touch U' (Allen/Clark/Collen/Elliott/Lange)
Based on a line lifted from 'Photograph', this trailing track is actually one of the freshest and most interesting on *Adrenalize*. It's singable, drenched in hooks and has those great harmonies, as well as a joyous delivery by Elliott and a playful solo from Collen. The worst that can be said about it is that it might be too pop – not exactly a scathing indictment, given Leppard's crossover track record.

'Tear It Down' (Clark/Collen/Elliott/Savage)
A recycled B-side from *Hysteria*'s US 'Women' and UK 'Animal' singles, this track cleaned up nicely to close *Adrenalize*. Filled with breathless, feral energy, it has the feel of early Leppard – a full-circle touchback to the band's youthful roots that is all too apropos, given that *Adrenalize* is closing out an era. What we really want and inexplicably don't get here is a blazing solo from Collen, which the tune is screaming for.

B-Sides
'You Can't Always Get What You Want' (Mick Jagger/Keith Richards)
This acoustic take on the Rolling Stones classic is a delightful departure from standard Leppard, featuring bluesy guitar work, a moody lead vocal reading from Elliott and big harmony vocals over a sparse instrumental track.

'Little Wing' (Jimi Hendrix)
This Hendrix cover has a late-night barroom feel, slow and soulful. Elliott's vocal is melancholy, and the percussion-free track is carried by an emotive piano; a synth flute stands in for the guitar lead.

'Tonight' (Clark/Collen/Elliott/Lange/Savage)
This demo version of the single features Steve Clark. The percussion is sparse through the first half of the song, as opposed to the finished version.

'Now I'm Here' (Brian May)
Recorded at the Freddie Mercury Tribute Concert on 20 April 1992 at Wembley Stadium, this spirited Queen track (penned by May) features lead solos from Collen, Campbell and May himself.

'Two Steps Behind' (Elliott)
This acoustic take on Elliott's ballad has an emphatic country feel, intentionally sparse and simple. Elliott's vocal is earnest; the harmonies are powerful, but don't overwhelm him. The guitar break evokes American country rocker Tim McGraw.

'Tonight' (Clark/Collen/Elliott/Lange/Savage)
Like the demo version, this take on 'Tonight' is all-acoustic and subdued. It was recorded at Sun Studio, Memphis, Tennessee, in February 1993.

'Too Late For Love' (Clark/Elliott/Lange/Savage/Willis)
From the *In The Round, In Your Face Tour* (February 1988), recorded live in Denver, Colorado. It features spectacular guitar work from Collen and Clark.

'Women' (Elliott/Savage/Collen/Clark/Lange)
Also from the Denver concert on the 1988 *In The Round, In Your Face Tour*. The acoustics are cavernous – Elliott's vocals are explosive as a result.

Retro Active (1993)

Personnel:
Joe Elliott: lead and backing vocals, piano, rhythm guitar
Rick Savage: bass, vocals, keyboards, rhythm guitar
Rick Allen: drums, percussion
Phil Collen: lead and rhythm guitars, backing vocals
Steve Clark: guitars
Vivian Campbell: electric and acoustic guitars, backing vocals
Robert 'Mutt' Lange, P.J. Smith: backing vocals
Fiachna Ó Braonáin: tin whistle
Ian Hunter, Liam Ó Maonlaí, Pete Woodroffe: piano
Peter O'Toole: mandolin
Recorded at Wisseloord Studios (Hilversum, Netherlands), Rainbow Studios
(Munich, Germany), Olympiahalle (Munich, Germany), Bow Lane Studios
(Dublin, Ireland) and Joe's Garage (Dublin, Ireland) between 1984 and 1993
Producer: Def Leppard, Pete Woodroffe
Engineers: Janfred Arendsen, Albert Boekholt, Freek Feenstra, Nigel Green, Steve
McGaughlin, Erwin Musper, Ronald Prent, Robert Scovill, Mike Shipley, Pete
Woodroffe
Released: 4 October 1993
Label: Mercury
Certification: Platinum (US)
Chart activity: US *Billboard* 200: 9, UK Albums: 6
Running time: 56:04

Strictly speaking, *Retro Active* is a compilation album, not a studio album. But
it isn't just a dumping ground for previously recorded tracks; there is fresh
work here, and some of it is significant in Leppard's development. It's
included in this studio album sequence for several reasons: compilation
album or not, it contains recordings done specifically for the album; it is the
last album to feature studio performances by Steve Clark; it is the first album
to feature studio performances by his replacement, Vivian Campbell; and it
contains the first album presentation of one of the band's most enduring
songs from the 1990s.

When Vivian Campbell joined Leppard, he had a greater rock pedigree than
all of his bandmates combined, by far. While he was a Leppard contemporary
(born in 1962), he was the first non-British member, being a native of
Northern Ireland. He'd stepped into Dio to replace Jake E. Lee when the latter
had stepped into Ozzy Osbourne's band to replace the deceased Randy
Rhodes before joining David Coverdale's Whitesnake in 1987.

When Leppard made the decision to replace Clark (after briefly considering
continuing as a four-piece), Campbell was one of five guitarists considered
(Iron Maiden's Adrian Smith being one of the others). Campbell won the post
as much for his strength as a singer as for his guitar-playing. Collen stated in

his autobiography that Campbell was the final step in the band's quest to make their live vocals as full as their studio vocals. '[Viv] is technically … the best singer in the band', Collen wrote. 'I remember the first time [he sang with us in a studio], at a BBC radio session, hearing the backing vocals the three of us had just done, thinking they sounded so good that they must be a sample.'

He was the right guy at the right time, and remains a Leppard to this day, having put in 30 years of service – ironically, the same length of time that Steve Clark walked the earth.

Much of the album consists of B-sides accumulated from previous albums, but there are some other gems, including outtakes that were unfinished and set aside during the recording of previous albums but were completed for this one, as well as some alternate versions.

'[Def Leppard's] chief strength has always been the songs they write, and *Retro Active* underscores that appeal', wrote Paul Evans in *Rolling Stone*. 'From the Zep-like 'Desert Song' to 'She's Too Tough' and its feisty rock 'n' roll, from the power ballad 'Two Steps Behind' to 'Ride Into The Sun', a raver from their 1979 debut, this is premium pop-metal – sharp hooks and engaging thunder.'

'This is an interesting release which marks the end of a long chapter in the band's history, following the death of guitarist and guiding force Steve Clark', wrote Eduardo Rivadavia in *Allmusic*. 'While casual fans might find it confusing, Leppard fanatics will revel in its diversity and informative liner notes.'

Writing years later, *Sputnikmusic* noted that '*Retro Active* cannot be rated super highly; it is extremely rare for a compilation album such as this to do so. With that in mind, this is indeed a pleasant surprise which will at least please some of Def Leppard's longtime fans due to the relatively organic production levels used here.'

The album went to number nine on the US *Billboard* 200 chart and number six on the UK Albums chart.

Cover Art

For a decade, Andie Airfix had provided the cover design and art for Leppard's studio product. This time out, it fell to Nels Israelson and Huge Syme, who provided a photograph of a woman sitting at a dressing table with a large mirror. The image doubles, however, as a skull, reflecting the album's dark tone.

'Desert Song' (Clark/Elliott/Savage)
Released as a single in November 1993
Charts: US *Billboard* Mainstream Rock: 12
Originally conceived as an instrumental track for *Hysteria,* the song was shelved for years before Elliott picked it up again on an off-day during the *Adrenalize* tour. It's one of the last Leppard tracks released to include the compositional input and recorded guitar tracks by Steve Clark. Clark's

replacement, Vivian Campbell, provides backing vocals, making 'Desert Song' the only Leppard tune on which they both perform.

Elliott's lyric was spurred by the ill health of British rockmeister Mick Ronson, one of his idols, who was battling liver cancer at the time and died soon after. The lyric is about facing death alone.

The second single released from the album, it reached number 12 on the US *Billboard* Mainstream Rock chart.

'Fractured Love' (Clark/Elliott/Savage)

Another unfinished *Hysteria* track, 'Fractured Love' is an exceptionally powerful track, uncharacteristically dark and tense. A radical departure from the boy-longs-for-girl theme, it's about the emotional anguish of a failed relationship, one of the moodiest songs in the Leppard canon. As such, it wouldn't have fit in with *Hysteria*'s vibe at all. It's not just the subject matter that departs from Leppard's business-as-usual template; the song's structure is likewise unique, built on one repeating rhythm and a single musical phrase. Its shadowy, subdued tone (largely created by Collen playing with an e-bow), with Elliot's low, whispered vocal, goes on for a full two minutes before the band finally explode into view, becoming their usual crunchy selves.

The intro and drums were re-recorded for the *Retro* version, but the lead solo by Clark was retained from the *Hysteria* sessions. It is uncharacteristically restrained, but the melody conveys the longing and pain of the story Elliott is telling.

'Action' (Brian Connolly/Andy Scott/Steve Priest/Mick Tucker)

Released as a single on 3 January 1994

Charts: US *Billboard* Hot 100: 20, UK Singles chart: 15

If *Retro* is a grab bag, 'Action' might be the most random thing in it: it's a cover of The Sweet's 1975 hit single, a runaway rocker that the guys in Leppard had loved as young teenagers.

The track came to life as a B-side for 'Make Love Like A Man' the previous year, prior to Campbell coming on board, and was touched up for its new deployment: Allen re-recorded the snare drum, and Campbell dropped in fresh background vocals alongside P.J. Smith.

'Andy [Scott, lead guitarist of Sweet] said that our version of 'Action' was the best cover of a Sweet song he'd ever heard', Elliott told Dave Ling in *Classic Rock*. It was so good, in fact, that it was released as the album's third and final single in January 1994, hitting number 14 on the UK Singles chart – one notch above The Sweet's version.

'Two Steps Behind' (Acoustic) (Elliott)

Released as a single on 24 August 1993

Charts: US *Billboard* Mainstream Rock: 5, US *Billboard* Hot 100: 12, US *Billboard* Mainstream Top 40: 5, UK Singles chart: 32

If 'Action' is *Retro's* most random track, 'Two Steps Behind' is the most unlikely. It's a ballad that, in its first release, was more a country track than a rock track – and yet it's Leppard, through and through.

Written solely by Elliott in 1989, as the band were beginning to plan the recording of *Adrenalize,* it wound up shelved, despite a demo that was electric, not acoustic. Three years later, Elliott reintroduced it during a jam session to come up with B-sides for the *Adrenalize* singles. It was paired with 'Make Love Like A Man', but the band recording was done entirely acoustically – a Leppard first – at Collen's suggestion.

Early the following year, the producers of the movie *Last Action Hero* contacted the band and asked for a song to use in the film. Still on tour, they couldn't stop to record anything new, but offered 'Two Steps Behind'. Film composer Michael Kamen took the acoustic tapes and added soaring, atmospheric strings, and it became that film's closing credits music. That's the version presented first on *Retro.*

The song is gentle and somewhat melancholy, an earnest expression of devotion and the perseverance of love – again, not exactly a stock Leppard sentiment, but a very commendable one. There are no rhythm tracks – just guitars and voices, the latter reliably harmonising angelically. Collen's lead solo is likewise acoustic, evoking the early Eagles.

So well did it turn out that it became the first single released from *Retro,* ascending to number five on both the US *Billboard* Mainstream Rock and Top 40 charts, number 12 on the *Billboard* Hot 100 and, surprisingly, number 29 on the US *Billboard* Adult Contemporary chart. It reached number 32 on the UK Singles chart.

An electric version was also recorded and appears near the end of *Retro.*

'She's Too Tough' (Elliott)

As this track opens, Leppard channel the early 1970s Hollies, but in no time, they've turned into Mötley Crüe, with Elliott reaching into an unkempt Vince Neil screech and Collen serving up standard Mick Mars crunch. If that was all that was happening, the song would be dismissible, but there are some of those delightfully drastic key changes to keep the ear amused, and some wonderful 1960s pop callback harmonies of the sort Extreme had used the previous year on 'Warheads'. Collen's solo is as over-the-top as he's ever been, and he scrapes like he's auditioning for Boston.

The song had actually been written eight years earlier and handed off to Helix, who put it on their *Wild In The Streets* album in 1987.

'Miss You In A Heartbeat' (Acoustic) (Collen)

Released as a single in December 1993
Charts: US *Billboard* Hot 100: 39
Like Elliott before him, Phil Collen stepped up with this just-me composition written in 1991 and recorded by the momentary Paul Rodgers band The Law.

He was writing about his son, Rory, and told *Songfacts* that it had emerged out of missing his family when he was on the road with the band.

The band recorded their own version the following year and put it on the B-side of the 'Make Love Like A Man' single (that version, which is standard Leppard, is presented below). This acoustic version, however, is a gentle piano ballad (Leppard's first). It was added to the album when Elliott heard Collen noodling around on a piano and did his own demo of it, which grew into this acoustic version. The piano part in the final track was played by Pete Woodroffe.

Released as the album's second single in June 1993, it went to number 39 on the US *Billboard* Hot 100.

'Only After Dark' (Mick Ronson/Scott Richardson)

This Mick Ronson cover (from his 1974 debut album Slaughter On 10th Avenue) is a homage to a Leppard hero. The band grew up on Ronson's albums and adored him. Their version had been the B-side to the 'Let's Get Rocked' single the previous year, with extra guitar added here. The track is lovingly rendered, eschewing the usual Leppard ornaments for straight-up, four-on-the-floor rock.

'Ride Into The Sun' (Elliott/Savage/Collen/Clark)

This new version of one of their earliest tunes is an unexpected innovation and a fun surprise. Where the original track had been dark and heavy, this one is downright jaunty – a shift that's immediately apparent in the 1950s rock 'n' roll piano intro by Ian Hunter. The rest of the new version had been laid down in 1987 during the *Hysteria* sessions, but the intro featured a Rick Allen drum solo (which Hunter's piano intro replaced). The rest of the drum tracks were re-recorded as well.

'From The Inside' (Elliott)

Easily the most out-of-place track on the album, this song backed the 'Have You Ever Needed Someone So Bad' single from the previous year. An acoustic ballad that seems more appropriate for a folk music festival than a hard rock album, it features a piano, tin whistle and mandolin, all played by guest performers.

Elliott labours manfully to sound authentic, and the rest of the band manage to rein themselves in (a testament to the solid training in sonic dynamics they received from Mutt Lange). Although it adds still more variety to an already-diverse album, it just doesn't fit.

'Ring Of Fire' (Clark/Collen/Elliott/Lange/Savage)

On the one hand, this frenetic rocker recalls the energy of the band's pre-Collen-and-Campbell early years; on the other, it has the sheen of the mid-1980s Mutt Lange era. It's perfectly serviceable, but doesn't stand out.

Originally recorded during the *Hysteria* sessions and slapped on the back of the 'Pour Some Sugar On Me' single (in the US) and the 'Armageddon It' single (in the UK), it was partially re-recorded for *Retro*. Rick Savage played rhythm guitar, and Mutt Lange sang backing vocals.

'I Wanna Be Your Hero' (Elliott/Savage/Collen/Clark/Lange)
With an opening that recalls earlier ballads, this track cranks up rapidly after a few remorseful clean-guitar measures, shifting to chunky-dirty guitars and a powerful rhythm. There are some satisfying modulations, beautifully layered guitars and a terrific Steve Clark solo. It sounds very Hysteria, and sure enough, it was the B-side of 'Animal' (in the US) and 'Pour Some Sugar On Me' (in the UK). The ballad-like intro was added for this version, and the drums were re-recorded. (Interesting bit of trivia: this track was originally called 'Love Bites', but Mutt Lange stole that title for the song he contributed to Hysteria – so the song was retitled 'I Wanna Be Your Hero'.)

'Miss You In A Heartbeat' (Electric) (Collen)
This fully-electric version of 'Miss You In A Heartbeat' isn't as emotive as the acoustic version, but the guitars are reliably diverse and well-layered, with great juxtaposition of dirty and clean. This one plods a little bit, but is nonetheless a fine track.

'Two Steps Behind' (Electric) (Elliott)
At just under nine minutes in length, this electric version of Elliott's signature ballad is more than twice the length of the acoustic version. But that's a fake-out; the electric version is just a few seconds shorter, and the extra length is given over to Elliott's piano-and-voice demo of 'Miss You In A Heartbeat'.

That's a delightful surprise because the demo is beautiful, and the lyrics come across with an undeniable tenderness when all the noise is stripped away. It's also a bit of a relief because the electric version of 'Two Steps Behind' is disappointing; the song needs to be an acoustic ballad, and even if it could be dressed in full Leppard regalia, it certainly didn't happen here. The guitars lack any innovation, and Elliott struggles to get the emotion across in the overly busy mix. The hidden demo fully redeems him.

Slang (1996)

Personnel:
Joe Elliott: lead and backing vocals, rhythm guitar, bass
Rick Savage: bass, synth bass, vocals, acoustic guitar
Rick Allen: drums, percussion
Phil Collen: lead and rhythm guitars, mandolin, backing vocals
Vivian Campbell: electric and acoustic guitars, dulcimer, backing vocals
Pete Woodroffe: piano, synthesiser strings
Ram Narayan, Shyam Vatish: sārangā
Av Singh: Dohl
Gloria Flores: vocals
Recorded at 'A house in Spain' (Marbella, Spain) and Bow Lane Studios (Dublin, Ireland) between 1994 and 1996
Producers: Pete Woodroffe, Def Leppard
Engineers: Pete Woodroffe, Ger McDonnell
Released: 13 May 1996
Label: Mercury
Certification: Gold (US), Gold (UK)
Chart activity: UK Albums: 5, US *Billboard* 200: 14
Running time: 45:58

All great bands reinvent themselves at some point. The Van Halen that recorded *5150* was not the band that recorded *Women And Children First;* the Pink Floyd that recorded *The Wall* was not the Pink Floyd that recorded *The Piper At The Gates Of Dawn*. And The Beatles, of course, reinvented themselves with every single album.

Now it was Def Leppard's turn, for some of the same reasons – the passage of time and new blood in the band, to name a couple. Steve Clark was now five years gone, and Vivian Campbell had been a Leppard for most of those years. And a full *nine* years had passed since *Hysteria*. Put simply, Leppard had little choice but to reinvent themselves; they had transitioned from gods to jokes, where the radio was concerned. It was once fashionable to worship Leppard; now it was fashionable to hate them. In all fairness, that was true of many if not most bands of the MTV era. Grunge was now firmly entrenched, and hair metal looked goofy and a little fey standing next to it. On the other hand, when *Adrenalize* had circled the globe, those conditions already existed – grunge had displaced hair metal, and Leppard's traumas had already happened. But despite this, *Adrenalize* had been kept in the air by a hugely successful world tour; fashion and trauma aside, Leppard knew how to put on a show.

Still, there was more going on at this point, much of it very personal. Joe Elliott and Phil Collen were both going through divorces; Rick Savage was struggling with Bell's Palsy, and his father passed away; Elliott and Rick Allen had both been arrested for spouse abuse. But now they could actually write and sing about what they were feeling. Mutt Lange, who would have forbidden that sort of thing, was – for the first time in 15 years – nowhere to be found. Lange's absence also prompted a departure from the ultra-slick, ultra-shiny sonic production that had defined the band. 'We'd got so sick of recording the old way. We didn't want to do it anymore', Savage told Jerry Ewing in *Metal Hammer*. 'We wanted the music to be more personalised and let the character of the individuals come out.'

'At least it gave us the chance to grow up a little', said Vivian Campbell of the first studio album in which he was a full participant. 'We live in a state of arrested development in this band, singing songs like 'Let's Get Rocked'. So, we did get to write some grown-up lyrics.'

Phil Collen cited a return to early influences as another big motivator in an interview on the band's website, calling the album 'a hybrid of our favourite bands: the rock of Led Zeppelin, the glam of David Bowie, the coolness of T. Rex. That really still motivates us.' And they certainly couldn't go with the grunge flow. 'We couldn't just go out there and make an album sounding like Nirvana. That'd be ridiculous', Elliott said in an interview on *The Lep Report*. 'That would have been like cashing in, bandwagon-style. But what we did do was just strip back a lot of the harmony stuff and just make a much more lyrically honest record.'

The pulling back of the trademark harmonies contributed to the album's raw sound, and though there's plenty of satisfying back-and-forth between Collen and Campbell, the band also brought in exotic instruments that were light-years from any definition of hard rock – such as the sārangī, a South Asian stringed instrument, and the dohl, an Indian percussion instrument.

All this change, however, was just too much for Leppard's audience. *Slang* didn't go beyond gold in either the UK or the US, making it the first Leppard album ever to fail to achieve platinum status in the latter. It was also the first album since *High 'N' Dry* to do better in the UK than in the US. Three of the album's four singles failed to chart at all in the US.

'It's funny – at the time, *Slang* was deemed 'not good enough'', Elliott told *Rolling Stone*. 'But we couldn't have made another like *Adrenalize*. It would have killed us. We had already done the big trilogy of albums with massive productions, and we had to go back and start again from zero. And I think this is the most honest record we've ever made. By the time we got to the studio to do it, we collectively started getting married, we started getting divorced, parents started passing away and kids were being born. All of a sudden, we woke up into reality. And we decided to write about it. People weren't ready for that. But to churn out a batch of insignificant rock songs in 1996 would have been an even bigger mistake.'

'Nirvana had come along and everything had changed', Phil Collen told *Billboard*. 'I think we could've put out *Sgt. Pepper's* or *Dark Side Of The Moon,* and [still] gotten lumped in with all the crap metal bands of the 1980s that were kind of pale versions of us. *Slang* was an essential album for Def

Leppard. It went against the grain [but] we felt like *Adrenalize* started turning a little bit similar, so it was important to do something different at that point.'

By eschewing both their hair metal legacy and a me-too bow to grunge, going into uncharted waters, they would alienate some of their fan base and likely do very badly financially. They did it anyway, privately giving *Slang* the working title of *Commercial Suicide.* The album was, as reinventions go, exactly what Leppard was striving for. But it was not a success.

Even so, *Rolling Stone*'s Jon Wiederhorn gave Leppard the benefit of the doubt. 'In the 1980s, Def Leppard's extravagant productions and power-rock anthems prompted a generation to empty its pockets and unzip its pants in pursuit of pop nirvana', he wrote. 'But today's listeners want more than cheap thrills and stomping sing-alongs. To comply, the band have stripped down their booming sound and expanded their musical vocabulary.' Stephen Thomas Erlewine, writing for *Allmusic,* was likewise positive: 'Def Leppard haven't sounded so immediate since *Pyromania.*'

The *Encyclopaedia Metallum* wasn't so kind: '*Slang* is an album full of boring radio pop. There are so many slow songs on the album that it's irritating even to think of listening to it straight through.' *Q Magazine* was more understanding, proposing that the problem wasn't so much Leppard as the genre, concluding that the album was 'the work of a huge band, aware that the straight-ahead rock they once plied so enthusiastically is dead and who have embraced the new breed with élan.'

Cover Art

The scrapping of Leppard tradition continued with the album's cover art. Missing, for the first time ever, was the band's triangular logo. In its place was a sleek, understated logo, concocted by Jager di Paolo, above a snakish rendering of the album's title over the shadowy, downcast face of an Indian woman, showing a starry blue *Bindi* mark on her forehead and binary digits all over the place. Not exactly a head-banging inducement, but certainly more complex and mysterious than the band's previous covers.

'Truth?' (Campbell/Collen/Elliott/Savage)

From the first five seconds of the song, you know we're not in Kansas anymore. This is not like any Leppard we've ever heard before. Sure enough, the big harmonies are gone; the production is raw, far from the band's pristine standard, and it's a full 45 seconds before the band get around to playing a second chord. There is *nothing* about this song that says 'Def Leppard'.

The song delivers on the broader promise of more adult themes. Elliott is confronting the complexity of the world, seeing a lot of moral compromise and searching for the truth. He's encouraging the listener to question everything and to take a stand against the world's deceptions. All of that might be an even tougher pill for the band's fanbase to swallow than the change in sound.

The guitars aren't layered at all – a disappointment, since we rapidly find on tracks to follow that they haven't forgotten how – but that's not as jarring as hearing Rick Allen hitting an actual snare drum, rather than a digital pad, for the first time in over a decade. It all somehow works, though, and when the song completely changes rhythm and key, from F# to B, a little over two minutes in, the familiarity of that move adds to the power mix of elements here: yes, it doesn't sound like Def Leppard, but it definitely *is* Def Leppard.

'Turn To Dust' (Collen)

If 'Truth?' had signalled that a new Leppard was coming through the door, 'Turn To Dust' screamed it from the rooftops. The Indian instruments are certainly the biggest divergence; in the first five seconds of the tune, we feel like we're in a Beatles session in 1967. And they don't skimp; the sārangī and the dohl, played by Indian musicians, are all-pervasive, utterly inhabiting the song. And ... slide guitar?

Still, there are some very Leppard-like traits in evidence: Allen's drum intro echoes Led Zeppelin, one of the band's key influences, and at the chorus, the key shifts unexpectedly (Indian music typically remains in one key) from C to Bb.

The sonic disorientation here is so great that the lyrics and their meaning might have to fight their way into the listener's attention, but again, this ain't your big brother's Leppard: this song is *about something*.

> Slave or sympathy it atrophies
> Save the ancient hearts
> Hiding scars and knives in symphonies
> Still we rise to fall

The theme is disconnection, feeling adrift and pummeled by change. This is exactly how we might expect the band to feel after living through the events of the previous few years. The lyrics go on to express vulnerability, even a kind of existential dread, and acknowledge that we tend to cover up those feelings.

The Indian adornment of the music completes the emotional tone of the song perfectly – just as it did when The Beatles used it, creating resonance rather than simply leaning on harmony. Overall, a strange, disruptive track, but a really good one.

'Slang' (Collen/Elliott)

Released as a single in May 1996
Charts: UK Rock & Metal: 1, UK Singles chart: 17
A lot about Leppard is different on this album, but the title track reminds us of who they are: it's a short-and-sweet celebration of phone sex, up-tempo and raucous. Showcasing another Joe Elliott innuendo catalogue, for the first

time ever, Elliott actually raps. Anyone who finds that troubling will be grateful that the song is mercifully short.

It was the album's lead single, topping the UK Rock & Metal chart and going to number 17 on the UK Singles chart.

'All I Want Is Everything' (Elliott)
Released as a single in August 1996
Charts: UK Rock & Metal: 2, UK Singles chart: 38
Listenable but certainly not remarkable, this Elliott-only composition is as moody as Leppard fans expect him to be, but doesn't go too far. The structure of the song is borderline monotonous, almost country in its feel, but the song has Leppard-ish dynamics, rising and falling to increase emotional tension, which enhances its listenability. Collen serves up a poignant solo towards the end that is notable for its minimalist economy.

The lyric's sombre-but-frantic tone is best appreciated through the lens of the band's troubles during this period; Elliott describes feeling stuck in a relationship that has stalled, a reflection of the band's domestic struggles with divorce and parenthood at the time.

It was the album's third single.

'Work It Out' (Campbell)
Released as a single in July 1996
Charts: UK Rock & Metal: 1, UK Singles chart: 22, US *Billboard* Mainstream Rock: 6
New Leppard Vivian Campbell co-wrote *Slang*'s opening track, but this cut is his first sole-composer credit. It has a touch of the industrial feel of that earlier track, with a factory-steady *thump-bang* from Allen – all the more effective on a semi-acoustic drum kit – and a bass riff from Savage that thrums like a revving motor. It's an attention-grabbing piece, musically slam-dunking the less-1980s sound the band were striving for. The guitars are delay-heavy, nodding to Leppard's past, and the bridge is stunning, with wah-wah bass and a simple and steady backing – and no real lead. It's all mood, brilliantly rendered.

The lyric is cafe-at-one-am philosophy, a reflection on isolation and alienation that manages to maintain a positive thread. Elliott sells it intuitively, singing the entire song at the bottom of his register. Overall, this track sounds *nothing* like Leppard, but it is utterly impressive.

It was the album's second single.

'Breathe A Sigh' (Collen)
Released as a single in November 1996
Charts: UK Rock & Metal: 1, UK Singles chart: 43
Elliott's 'Two Steps Behind' had proven beyond doubt that Leppard could deliver in acoustic mode, and this Phil Collen ballad became the next experiment in that vein. The melodic guitar lines have a distinctly R&B feel,

but the structure of the song is straight-up country. The lyrics aren't brilliant, but the layered harmonies are breathtaking: they are stacked high and deep, and the band confessed that Boyz 2 Men had inspired that move. More power to 'em – it works. The lead guitar work is clean and bluesy.

The song is admirable for its restraint, yet it still contains innovations that are stirring – an inspired modulation from D major to B major in the bridge and a sonic drop-out in the coda – making it fresh and interesting. It's another successful track in the album's not-your-father's-Leppard column.

It was the album's fourth and final single, and should have performed better than it did.

'Deliver Me' (Elliott/Collen)

This rocker recalls Nirvana – alternating between dark/quiet and loud/angry. It's an odd choice on an album that is supposedly going out of its way to avoid grunge, but the song works, even if it's out of place. Collen's solo is an early-1970s throwback, and Elliott repeats his low-register crawl, both to great effect.

'Gift Of Flesh' (Collen)

The album's other rocker contributes nothing to its let's-try-something-new ambition; it is, if anything, a homage to Leppard 1979, with loud and fast guitars, a clever modulation and a lyric that's joyfully over the top. It's a riff-ridden rock-out, intense and unapologetic, and the solo wails.

'Blood Runs Cold' (Collen/Elliott)

Like *Adrenalize*'s 'White Lightning' before it, 'Blood Runs Cold' pays homage to Steve Clark, five years gone when this track was recorded. The song captures the band's emotions at the time when Clark was falling into his abyss, and Elliott's vocal projects both sorrow and determination.

The guitar work is beautiful and melancholy without being mournful. Collen, who likened the backing music to the early work of the Police, explained to *Songfacts* that its middle eight was suggested by producer Pete Woodroffe, who thought that dropping in a female vocal alongside Elliott might be effective, in the tradition of Pink Floyd's *Dark Side Of The Moon*. Collen himself recorded a guide vocal for that part, and they liked it so much that they just left it in. He also praised Savage's bass track.

'Where Does Love Go When It Dies' (Collen/Elliott)

The title is goofy, but this ballad's introspective vibe and acoustic atmosphere are a highlight of the album, as they tip their hat to U2 and a host of other predecessors with this sadly philosophical exercise. Musically, it has more substance than 'Breathe A Sigh' – boomy kick drum intro, echoing, atmospheric guitar, sparse backing over Joe's wistful vocal – but it shares that song's earnest demeanour.

'Pearl Of Euphoria' (Collen/Elliott/Savage)
This final track ends Slang in good faith, very much in keeping with its try-new-things mission. The song is a distinctly non-Leppard exercise, built around a single chord and an unwavering bass note – not unlike The Beatles' 'Tomorrow Never Knows', but tasting very much like late-1980s U2. It's an aggressive work of relentless pulse and huge guitars, leaning toward Led Zeppelin in its drawn-out fade, invoking a bluesy psychedelia (Collen and Campbell volley back and forth, which is a real treat). Elliott's lyrics are inscrutable, but he delivers one last vocal experiment as he goes dreamy and angsty at the same time. It's a perfect conclusion to the album, enough to make the listener break out headphones and burn some incense.

Japanese Bonus Track
'Move With Me Slowly' (Collen)
'This one is probably my favourite', Elliott told *Rolling Stone.* 'It's one of Phil's songs, and it's very Stones-y. There's some lovely guitar work on it, and I think it had a lot to do with the way the current album turned out. Unfortunately, not that many people have heard it, though.'
    The track also appears on the 2014 Deluxe Edition.

B-Sides
'Animal' (Elliott/Savage/Collen/Clark/Lange)
This 1995 acoustic reading of 'Animal' isn't nearly as well-developed as most other Leppard acoustic remakes; it's essentially a straight-up copy of the original, with acoustic guitars swapped out for the electric guitars. The raucous energy that inhabited the original is consequently missing; the song can't do without the feral guitar howls that defined it.

'Ziggy Stardust' (David Bowie)
An acoustic take on the Bowie classic, this track has rougher edges than the original, which has a bright, polished sheen. It works for Leppard here because they are generally not musical storytellers, and this is a story song; their stripped-down, almost country approach to the tune makes it seem folksy and easier to absorb.

'Pour Some Sugar On Me' (Elliott/Savage/Collen/Clark/Lange)
As mentioned above, Elliott originally conceived 'Pour Some Sugar' as a country tune. Here, in this acoustic version, they get back to that, at least somewhat; the guitars are certainly more backporch-sounding, but Allen's straight-ahead rhythm and Elliott's powerhouse vocal delivery are held over from the rowdy original.

'Work It Out' (Campbell)
The album version of this track was Campbell's first stand-alone contribution to the Leppard canon, and this demo version gives insight into the band's

studio process on *Slang*. The song's foundation in both versions is a nervous techno-pop tempo, an ethereal buzzing here as opposed to a slicker, edgier sound in the finished track. Elliott's vocal is dreamier here, and an octave doubling of his voice on the chorus gives the track an atmosphere that was excised for the final version.

'Truth?' (Campbell/Collen/Elliott/Savage)
This original demo for the album track displays much of what appears in the final version, but is more drawn out (by nearly two minutes); the intro is much longer, there's an extra section before the lead, an additional chorus and yet another segment before the final chorus.

'Move With Me Slowly' (Collen)
Written for the *Slang* album, it was relegated to B-side/bonus track status despite its musical quality and strong performances all around. It's true the band were going for a different sound on *Slang*, but Elliott's vocal is the only Leppard-sounding thing about it. Even Collen's guitar work sounds more like Journey's Neal Schon than Phil Collen.

'Two Steps Behind' (Live Acoustic) (Elliott)
The acoustic version of 'Two Steps Behind' became (and remains) a signature Leppard concert staple, more than three decades on from *Retro Active*. This live performance (on which Elliott himself performs) is representative of the song as it reads from the stage: intimate, heartfelt, unforced. (Recorded in Singapore.)

''Cause We've Ended As Lovers' (Stevie Wonder)
It's a Stevie Wonder tune, but this mournful rendition by Leppard was birthed as an offering to the Jeff Beck tribute album *Jeffology: A Guitar Chronicle*. The restless, moody lead work is Collen's, earnest in the looseness with which he plays (he is typically far tighter and more controlled). In the song's second half, he does revert more to his own style, continuing the homage with soaring peak notes that echo the wailing lamentation of Beck's original track.

'Led Boots' (Max Middleton)
Also from the Jeff Beck tribute album, this time it's Viv Campbell on lead. Rather than bluesing it up in Beck fashion as his colleague had done on the first half of ''Cause We've Ended As Lovers', Campbell indulges his own style from the outset; deeply enamoured by Beck's singular technique, he doesn't set out to imitate it.

'All I Want Is Everything' (Edit) (Elliott)
This version doesn't differ significantly from the album track; it's just 57 seconds shorter. The trims include two lines excised from the second verse and the second half of an extended outro with a Collen lead solo.

'When Saturday Comes'/'Jimmy's Theme' (Elliott)

Elliott wrote these two tracks for the Sean Bean film of the same name. The former is amiable but unremarkable; the latter is a slow, relaxed instrumental. Both tracks were performed by Elliott, Collen and Savage.

Euphoria (1999)

Personnel
Joe Elliott: lead and backing vocals
Rick Savage: bass, vocals
Phil Collen: lead guitar, vocals
Rick Allen: drums
Vivian Campbell: lead guitar, vocals
Robert John 'Mutt' Lange: backing vocals
Damon Hill: guitar
Ciaran McGoldrick, Gary Sullivan, Ricky Warwick: 'hey's and claps
Recorded at Joe's Garage (Dublin, Ireland) between May 1998 and March 1999
Producers: Pete Woodroffe, Def Leppard
Engineers: Ronan McHugh, Ger McDonnell
Released: 8 June 1999
Label: Mercury
Certification: Gold (US)
Chart activity: US *Billboard* 200: 11, UK Rock & Metal Albums: 1, UK Albums: 11
Running time: 51:07

Converging circumstances had forced Leppard out of their comfort zone on *Slang,* spurring unprecedented inventiveness and experimentation – to the alienation of fans around the world. Still, they'd hung in there, and when that tour had ended and their disrupted lives settled back down, they found themselves in more familiar territory.

Grunge had flamed out early, restoring pop/rock to its rightful place in the radio firmament. The fanbase's feedback on *Slang* had strongly indicated that even if Leppard couldn't remain in the 1980s, there were elements of their sound that fans had simply come to expect. And the band itself – not the same band that had delivered *Pyromania* and *Hysteria* and *Adrenalize* – had grown solid and tight throughout the 1990s. Vivian Campbell, taking on the near-impossible task of replacing Steve Clark, had now held the post for seven years – half as long as Clark himself had.

Euphoria took shape in Joe Elliott's Dublin garage, over a period of ten months between 1998 and 1999. The band gave themselves permission to loosen up, to not be as focused on the vagaries of the rock market as they had been.

'When we came to do the *Euphoria* album, we started recording it in 1998, but we hadn't actually made a Def Leppard-sounding record since 1991', Elliott recalled. 'So, it had been a good eight years – which is just the exact amount of time The Beatles were together – since we'd made a classic Def Leppard record ... So, it felt very natural to go back to writing songs that were like the ones that we'd ... previously recorded. And this also coincided with what was happening with the music industry. It was moving away from the dark grunge towards a much more up-tempo, poppy kind of grunge music, if you like. With bands like Sugar Ray, who all started writing pop songs, you know. And so, taking that into consideration and our 'Okay, we got that thing out of our system', we were all starting to write songs that were happy. We just moved into that mood again. And so we had a lot of songs that were just rock. They just rocked. 'Demolition Man' and 'Back In Your Face'. Stuff like that.'

Mutt Lange even made an appearance, co-writing three of the album's tracks and contributing to the backing vocals. But he didn't sit back down in the producer's chair; that was occupied by Pete Woodroffe, with the band co-producing, as with *Slang*. Rick Allen recorded the drum parts in California so he could remain near his family.

The album included an instrumental track, Collen's 'Disintegrate' – the band's first instrumental in 18 years, since Steve Clark's 'Switch 625' from *High 'N' Dry*. It also featured a Vivian Campbell song (co-written with PJ Smith), 'To Be Alive', previously recorded and released by the band Clock.

Though the album was better received by both critics and fans, it still performed worse than *Slang* – in the UK, anyway, where the latter had at least gone gold, which *Euphoria* didn't. On the other hand, the lead single, 'Promises', gave the band another number-one hit on the US *Billboard* Mainstream Rock chart.

Over in the US, *Entertainment Weekly* liked it: 'Def Leppard are back in a big, bad *Hysteria*-sleek way.' *Rolling Stone*'s Greg Kot wasn't so impressed. 'Every multimillion-selling hack gets a second chance', he wrote. 'These blue-collar Brits have always been motivated by sales rather than art, so it's little wonder that they've abandoned the more introspective tone struck on *Slang* (1996), a commercial flop, to return to their 1980s metal-for-the-malls formula: hooks big enough to beach Moby Dick, lean arrangements that owe more to Thin Lizzy than to Black Sabbath and germ-free production that emphasises high-end sheen over low-end sludge. Old crony Mutt Lange takes time out from shepherding the career of his wife, Shania Twain, to lend a heavy hand on a couple of would-be hits, including 'Promises', which resurrects the 'Pour Some Sugar On Me' buzz. Yet, the defining characteristic of *Euphoria* is its bloodlessness, from the robotic drum tracks to the disconcertingly inhuman tone of those trademark massed vocal choruses. *Behind The Music* notwithstanding, the flesh-and-blood Def Leppard apparently never made it out of the 1980s alive.'

Allmusic's Stephen Thomas Erlewine was a little more balanced in his review, writing, 'From the outset, it's clear that *Euphoria* finds the band returning to the glam-inflected, unabashedly catchy, arena-ready pop-metal that made them stars – and it's also clear that they're not concerned with having a hit; they just want to make a good record. For them, that means returning to the pop-metal formula that made *Pyromania* and *Hysteria* blockbusters, even if they must know that this signature sound no longer guarantees a hit at the close of the 1990s. It is true that this approach means *Euphoria* sounds out of time in 1999, but it's a tight, attractive album with more than its share of big hooks, strong riffs and memorable melodies.'

Cover Art

Andie Airfix returned, submitting cover art in the classic Leppard tradition after the odd Middle Eastern-feeling *Slang* cover. It featured the triangular Leppard logo of old, backed by bright lights – simple yet familiar.

'Demolition Man' (Collen/Campbell/Elliott)

'Return to form' is the critic's cliché, and more than a few used it when they heard this opening track (though a few resorted to 'return to formula'). Yup, this is the Leppard of old: upbeat, hard-hitting, in-your-face, with scorching guitars, soaring harmonies, a signature guitar tone – Collen sounds like Collen again! – and very satisfying, out-of-the-blue modulations. And dumb lyrics.

That said, there's new stuff going on here: the song's breakneck pace recalls some of their childhood influences – The Sweet, in particular, with their affinity for fast tempos ('Ballroom Blitz', 'Action') – and the song is openly unpretentious, reflecting a sort of heightened self-awareness – or, alternately, an exuberant new sobriety – we hadn't seen before. And a guest guitarist! Savage invited his neighbour, Damon Hill, a Formula One racing champion, to sit in. The song should sound manufactured and self-indulgent, but instead comes across as fresh and invigorating.

'Promises' (Collen/Lange)

Released in May 1999 (US) and July 1999 (UK)
Charts: US *Billboard* Mainstream Rock: 1, UK Rock & Metal: 1, UK Singles chart: 41
This very strong second track was also the album's first single – an excellent choice, as it happened at a moment when the band had its Mutt on once again. Lange was back, albeit briefly, and not only co-wrote the tune with Collen but contributed backing vocals.

For this reason, we might casually assume it is bursting with Leppardness: juxtaposed lead and rhythm licks flow around delicious riffs (the opening one in particular) with powerful dynamics. The chorus is as glorious a hook as we've come to expect, and the harmonies soar unapologetically.

And the lyric? It's a song about relationship integrity. Not completely new for Leppard, but previously a rarity, and a welcome trend.

There's also a bit of self-quoting going on, according to Collen, who told *Billboard* that the band 'borrowed' some old licks from themselves: 'With 'Promises', I made the riff in the same key as 'Armageddon It' and 'Photograph'. It's basically a rip-off. If another band were to do that to us, we'd go, 'Jesus Christ, let's sue them!' But no one noticed.'

'Back In Your Face' (Elliott/Collen)

This track flips the sonic formula of the one before: when Elliott starts singing, everybody *but* Savage drops out; the aggressive, abrupt 'Hey!' chant and early chorus exposition puts the light on Elliott as he returns to his role as blue jean renaissance man, which was never convincing but always amusing. Consider it an authentication.

There's a great middle-eight that modulates off the map and the lyric serves up outlandish rhymes and audacious wordplay ('I can scare the pants off the holiest ghost'). The result is listenable and a lot of fun.

'Goodbye' (Savage)
Released as a single on 27 September 1999
Charts: UK Singles chart: 54

This token ballad, written by Savage alone, includes lots of Leppard hallmarks (warm, clean guitar intro; layered, moody backing in the verses; big dynamics shift at the end of each chorus). It is, all the same, an unremarkable exercise, recycling not only Leppard's own ballad canon but borrowing from their 1980s contemporaries. There are, however, two remarkable features to the tune: Campbell serves up a brief but superbly tasteful solo that is decidedly atypical, and Savage's lyric – like Collen's earlier 'Promises' – is a truly adult theme, focusing on commitment in the most earnest terms.

It was the album's third single, performing modestly (number 54 on the UK Singles chart, and not charting at all in the US).

'All Night' (Collen/Lange)
We learned from *Slang* that Mutt Lange had been a de-personalising force on Leppard, pushing back against songs that were too personal. Much of *Euphoria,* like its predecessor, shows Leppard's humanity emerging in the face of life's trials. This song is absolutely not one of them, perhaps due to Lange's brief influence. It is, in fact, a wholehearted nod to the band's most adolescent impulses in its previous work: 'All Night' means exactly that, and they're talking about (unsurprisingly) sex. Elliott is at his most seductive, and it's actually impressive that he manages to sound just as lascivious as ever in a vocal style he's never used before. That innovation is one of several that leave the tune, on balance, a winner: its sharp, economic rhythm and cleverly updated borrowings of 1970s guitar fills that recall both Bowie and ZZ Top, selective wah-wah and octave vocals that make it fresh and fun and yet another tune that's all Leppard while being all-new.

'Paper Sun' (Collen/Campbell/Elliott/Savage/Pete Woodroffe)
Released as a single in 1999
Charts: US *Billboard* Mainstream Rock: 11

One of the album's true highlights, this tune was team-composed (with an assist from producer Pete Woodroffe) and features great back-and-forth between Collen and Campbell, recalling the seamless partnership the former had with Steve Clark.

Collen's opening riff in G is plaintive, mournful and has a touch of the Middle East; a counterpoint riff comes in above it before Elliott's vocal begins

– just like old times. From there, the song is classic Leppard, with layered guitars and vocal counterpoint between the backing voices and Elliott that recalls 'Foolin'' – except that it remains in G through verse, bridge and chorus. An unexpected middle section takes up a new key, F#, and a stuttering rhythm, followed by a vocal middle-eight, and Campbell takes off with a frenetic, sky-high lead as Collen backs him with a syncopated fill. They trade places for the outro, Collen going on a more melodic excursion that careens between keys, from Bm to Dm to Cm to F – with the whole song ending on a ringing Em power chord.

In addition to being musically powerful in the best Leppard tradition, the song is the rare Leppard political commentary: it's about the Omagh car bombing, a terrorist incident that occurred in Northern Ireland in August 1998.

It was the album's second single – and perfect for that job – peaking at number 11 on the *Billboard* Mainstream Rock chart.

'It's Only Love' (Elliott/Lange/Savage/Campbell)
Listening to the album front to back, this song is jarring; it's a laid-back ballad (not a bad thing in itself), and as out of place as it's possible to be after the one-two punch of 'Paper Sun'. More jarring still is its radical departure from the Leppard ballad standard, better reflected in 'Goodbye': the song is lightly tinged with R&B, and sounds almost adult-contemporary in its warm, cooshy vibe. Lange pitched in on this one, so maybe it's on him, but it seems he'd have been much more likely to say, 'No, boys! Don't go there!' All of that said, the guitar work is once again admirably complementary, and the lyric is particularly poignant and insightful, a lover's earnest and vulnerable plea for understanding.

'21st Century Sha La La La Girl' (Collen/Elliott/Savage)
This sleek, club-ready, ultimately empty track is a throwback to 'Pour Some Sugar On Me', an exercise in ebullient superficiality that is pure pop fun but not at all rock. It restates Leppard's range while in no way extending it, and its only justification must be securing the band's slot in dance-floor songlists. That said, it does possess the subtle scent of redemption, in context: Leppard are declaring that they can still feel young when they try, despite the carnage of their 30s. Look for some decidedly retro guitar work that comes off as particularly joyous.

'To Be Alive' (Campbell/PJ Smith)
This smart, well-crafted track is a Vivian Campbell ballad first recorded by Clock, his side band (and co-written by bandmate PJ Smith). Its Leppardizing works well, as it naturally exploits all the band's ballad strengths: layered guitars, gentle intensity and, of course, the gorgeous ensemble vocals. Campbell's solo is restrained but poignant. In the end, it's not an amazing track, but it's certainly better than 'It's Only Love'.

'Disintegrate' (Collen)
For the first time in almost two decades, Leppard serve up an instrumental track. This Phil Collen extravaganza harnesses the muscularity of the band's heyday while showcasing his evolved tone (Campbell's, too, for that matter). Held up next to 'Switch 625', the last such excursion, it immediately suffers in comparison for its lack of complexity; on the other hand, the abrupt change-up in the middle, with an acoustic rhythm guitar appearing out of nowhere as the rhythm drops away, is both playful and interesting. It doesn't add a great deal to the album, but it's another reassurance that Leppard are feeling like their old selves again.

'Guilty' (Collen/Savage/Elliott/Campbell/Woodroffe)
Like 'Paper Sun', this strong track was a collaboration with producer Woodroffe and could well have been on *Hysteria* with its shifting keys, layered guitars, multiple sections and contrapuntal angel choir. Yet, it still sounds new, owing largely to the fresh, organic guitar tones served up by Collen and Campbell. Elliott's voice also displays some evolution here, as he lays down a lyric about confession and remorse that conveys sincerity. It's a shame this track wasn't a single.

'Day After Day' (Collen/Elliott/Campbell)
Released as a single on a tour promo disc on 8 June 1999
This unremarkable track is technically competent enough, but it's not much more than a recycling of all of Leppard's clichés, drowning in an inexplicable monotony. It does feature a decent lead break, an evocative dynamic drop-off before the final chorus and a spirited second lead break that continues over the final chorus.

   Even more inexplicable, it was the album's final single (though released only as a promotional single to DJs and reviewers, not as a commercial single).

'Kings Of Oblivion' (Elliott/Collen/Savage)
Frenetic, almost hypomanic, this closing track fulfils the album's promise of the same-but-different with its airtight rhythm, deeply integrated guitars and unexpected changes, while presenting a new Elliott vocal mode that might be called 'reporting on the world', and some drum tricks from Allen that seem tastefully exhumed from Supertramp. It's not enough to send the album out with a blaze of glory, but it feels good.

Japanese Bonus Track
'I Am Your Child' (Elliott/Collen/Savage)
This is the only appearance of this track by the three Leppard writers who teamed up to write 'Kings Of Oblivion'. It was never performed live. It's an upbeat, invigorating tune, a paean to romantic anticipation. Elliott's vocal on

the verses is low and suggestive, almost teasing. The guitar work has a biting edge, tense yet exuberant. It's vintage Leppard, though not really a standout track.

Australian Bonus Tracks
'Worlds Collide' (Elliott/Savage)
Taken from the B-side of the UK version of the single 'Promises', this track is musically and lyrically chaotic, conveying anxiety and desperation. Leppard are good at this sort of song, conveying tremendous tension and vulnerability, but this particular variation doesn't stand out; they'd already done a great many tracks like this.

'Under My Wheels' (Bruce/Dunaway/Ezrin)
This cover of an Alice Cooper track, originally a 1971 single from his album *Killer*, was cobbled together by Elliott and Collen, with contributions from Bob Kulick of KISS, Chuck Wright, Pat Torpey and Clarence Clemons (Springsteen's E Street Band), for the tribute album *Humanary Stew: A Tribute To Alice Cooper*. It's well-executed, intense but not overwhelming, but lacks the delicious anxiety of Cooper's original reading.

B-Sides
'Back In Your Face' (Elliott/Collen)
The album track, repurposed for inclusion with the single 'Promises'. (In the UK, this single was considered a double A-side.)

'Burnout' (Allen/Campbell/Elliott/Collen/Savage)
Leppard aren't given to excessive rhythmic experimentation, making this frenetic track an interesting departure; the energy of the rhythm guitar, which lays down a steady stream of crunchy 16th notes, carries the song. (The track was a leftover from the *Slang* sessions, and was reissued on the 2014 deluxe edition of the album. It was also used as the B-side of the 'Goodbye' international CD single.)

'Immortal' (Elliott)
Elliott's lyric teases at spiritual themes, unusual for him, as he works up a seductive rallying cry in pursuit of destiny. His philosophical questions are more interesting than the somewhat repetitive musical backing, which revisits the Hysteria days, conjuring nothing really new. Still a solid, competent tune.

'Who Do You Love?' (Ian Hunter)
From Hunter's first solo album (1975), following his departure from Mott the Hoople – an essential band in Leppard's formative years. This B-side to the single 'Goodbye' feels less organic than Hunter's original, which sounds personal and inviting; the Leppard take is solid but rendered more in party mode.

X (2002)

Personnel:
Joe Elliott: lead and backing vocals
Rick Savage: bass, vocals
Phil Collen: lead guitar, vocals
Rick Allen: drums
Vivian Campbell: lead guitar, vocals
Eric Carter: keyboards
Stan Schiller: guitar
Recorded at Joe's Garage (Dublin, Ireland), Polar Studios (Stockholm, Sweden) and Rumbo Studios (Los Angeles, California) between 2001 and 2002
Producers: Def Leppard, Per Aldeheim, Andreas Carlsson, Pete Woodroffe
Engineers: Stefan Glaumann, Richard Chycki, Ronan McHugh, Liz Sroka, Pete Woodroffe
Released: 30 July 2002
Label: Island (US), Mercury (UK)
Certification: none
Chart activity: US *Billboard* 200: 11, UK Rock & Metal Albums: 3, UK Albums: 14
Running time: 47:09

Slang had been a desperation move in a changing market, albeit one that gave Leppard a long-sought excuse for an artistically satisfying out-of-body experience. *Euphoria* had re-established their brand, but demonstrated that the world wasn't as enthralled with the brand as it had once been.

As the 21st century opened, then, the boys from Sheffield found themselves in an unusual position: their powers were undiminished, while their audience inevitably was, and they felt at long last a kind of permission to fully be themselves. And that meant writing and playing from where they were, as human beings, in the new millennium. They became adult musicians writing adult music for adult radio. *X,* their next album, was for all purposes an adult contemporary album.

X actually means *Ten* here, as in the Roman numeral, though it wasn't their tenth studio album; it was their eighth. They were counting *Retroactive* (which, though listed above, was technically a compilation album with lots of studio enhancement) and *Vault,* their first greatest hits collection.

'*Ten*'s a weird album,' Elliott is quoted on the band's website, 'because most people call it *X*. But I think we were at a crossroads with that album. We weren't really sure … Internally, we were all not going in the right direction. We had some discussions about how we should go.'

The biggest change was that the band brought in, for the first time, outside writers – an idea Elliott hated and to which he objected. But they gave it a try, bringing in American writer/producer Marti Frederiksen, who had worked with Aerosmith and Ozzy Osbourne, among others; Swedish songwriter/producers Per Aldeheim, Andreas Carlsson and Max Martin; and British songwriter/producers Wayne Hector and Steve Robson. These co-producers and co-writers were brought in for their pop sensibilities and broad experience in the pop market to help Leppard recraft their sound in a more commercial direction.

These guestwriter tunes are front-loaded into the first third of the album, giving the listener a somewhat unsettling feeling that they've put on the wrong record; in tone and theme, these five songs are all essentially essays on suburban romance. It's like Peter Cetera and Huey Lewis had a baby, and the baby wrote an album. We get lines like:

I need your love to fall in...
Had your name all tattooed on my heart...
Your light, won't you let it shine on me, yeah...
You showed me the way to love...
In every crowd, there's always someone with your face...

Pretty domestic stuff from the former gods of cock rock; it's just two steps away from yacht rock. And yet, these songs reflect the reality that enduring love and romantic renewal take work – lessons every generation needs to learn. So, props for that.

Yet perhaps the most notable new writing influence was Rick Allen, who hadn't written much of anything in his 20-plus years as a Leppard. This time around, he contributed to no less than ten of the album's 13 tracks.

Even so, the result underwhelmed Elliott: 'It's not a standout album', he said. 'I don't think it's a complete duffer, and it's certainly not *Hysteria*, but there is some good stuff on it.' The album did no better commercially or on the charts than *Euphoria* had done – but critics took positive notice (see below), calling it 'easily the most commercial album from the Lepps, more so than even *Adrenalize* or *Hysteria*' and 'they've decided to act their age.'

Commercial it most certainly is – *X* is brimming with tracks that are instantly likeable, tracks that are decidedly more pop than rock and unapologetically so. The production is reliably pristine, the band's performances characteristically formidable and, pop or not, the songs are still firmly guitar-grounded. But that's all quality; the substance of the songs took them right off rock radio and into the Adult Contemporary genre, where two of the album's three singles charted. The album itself went to number 11 on the US *Billboard* 200 chart, as *Euphoria* had, and number 14 on the UK Albums chart. But – for the first time in Leppard history – it earned no RIAA or OCC certifications at all.

'They adapt to global pop with their signature sound intact, and *X* may be their niftiest since *Adrenalize*', wrote Rob Sheffield in *Rolling Stone*.

'To their credit, they're not chasing the new, hip sound – no stabs at nu-metal or rap-rock here – but they've decided to act their age', wrote Stephen Thomas Erlewine in *Allmusic*. 'Unfortunately, that pretty much means they've left rock behind, turning out a bunch of even-handed adult-pop that is melodic without being tuneful, or memorable for that matter.'

Cover Art

The cover – a painted white X against a black background, with a barely visible Leppard logo to the side – was undistinguished, given the band's history of vivid, stylish presentation. On the other hand, the band photography was done by Clive Arrowsmith, who famously shot the cover of *Band On The Run*.

'Now' (Allen/Campbell/Collen/Elliott/Marti Frederiksen/Savage)

Released as a single on 5 August 2002
Charts: US *Billboard* Mainstream Rock: 26, US *Billboard* Adult Top 40: 40, UK Rock & Metal: 2, UK Singles chart: 23

Thirty seconds into this opening track, it seems like it could be a Tears for Fears track, or even U2 in an experimental mood: industrial rhythms and glassy sounds swirl around a guitar drone that slowly fades in, and it isn't until Elliott's voice emerges that it's even clear that it's Def Leppard. The explosive chorus, however, leaves no doubt. Allen and Savage erupt into the thunder we're used to, and Elliott – though more restrained than usual – sings with characteristic passion.

The track has the immediacy the lyric references, and the song's theme – acting with resolve – is deftly rendered by Elliott. The arrangement and production are filled with effective enhancements – dissonance in the lead break, dynamic dropouts with ethereal synthesiser echoes – that underscore the song's seriousness. It's an out-of-the-blue track, and one that takes some getting used to, but it's powerful.

'I see 'Now' as one of those great examples of meeting of the traditional thing and the contemporary sound that we are introducing on this record', Elliott said in notes on the band website.

It was the album's lead single, hitting number 26 on the US *Billboard* Mainstream Rock chart, number 40 on the US *Billboard* Adult Top 40 and number 23 on the UK Singles chart.

'Unbelievable' (Per Aldeheim, Andreas Carlsson, Max Martin)

Behold, the first song ever written specifically for a Def Leppard album that included not a single Leppard among its writers. This was quite a leap of faith for the band, but it worked out well: the song's wistful vibe – a product of its writers' pop genre acumen – may not be entirely familiar, musically, but it's a spot-on depiction of Leppard itself.

Power choruses in ballads were nothing new at the time – Leppard had helped set the standard – but to hear the band's signature sound beneath an adult contemporary lyric about sentimental longing works unusually well here. The middle eight and lead breaks are economical but ear-catching, and the final chorus modulation – up to A from G – while fairly conventional, is perfectly effective in Leppard's hands.

'You're So Beautiful' (Allen/Campbell/Collen/Elliott/Marti Frederiksen/Savage)
This energetic track is much more Leppard than the previous two – an across-the-board hook fest with a pulsing rhythm and sparse but tasteful backing under Elliott's invested delivery. It also reasserts the intricate arrangement for which the band are famous: unexpected, exhilarating modulations that surprise the ear and, of course, those marvellous vocal harmonies. The lead solo break returns the Leppard guitars of old, emphatic and aggressive, and the chorus chants feel like old friends.

'Everyday' (Allen/Campbell/Collen/Elliott/Marti Frederiksen/Savage)
Another ballad, and at this point, the total is already above the average for a Leppard record. This one starts out with a simple acoustic guitar, but it builds quickly into a smooth and layered tune, melodic and user-friendly – but more of a boy band tune than a Def Leppard track. Even so, the artful modulations between the verses, bridges and choruses are band-standard, seamless and fresh and exhilarating.

'Long, Long Way To Go' (Wayne Hector/Steve Robson)
Released as a single on 14 April 2003
Charts: US *Billboard* Adult Contemporary: 20
And still another ballad – as well as a second Leppard-free composition. Probably the least Leppard-like track on the album, this has not a single hallmark of the band's sound, possibly excepting the chorus vocals. It's a sad song, an expression of loss and remorse, well-rendered by Elliott and featuring exceptionally fluid bass work from Savage. There are classical guitar fills throughout, a rare and unexpected treat.

The track was the album's third and final single, notching a number 20 placement on the US *Billboard* Adult Contemporary chart.

'Four Letter Word' (Allen/Campbell/Collen/Elliott/Savage)
Released as a single on 23 November 2002
Charts: US *Billboard* Mainstream Rock: 30
Finally, a track written solely by the members of Leppard! The lyric is goofy, and rips off – of all people – Hall and Oates, but it wonderfully updates Leppard's adolescent sex themes in a cheeky way that acknowledges their status as parents of young children. A lone guitar, arhythmic and unsteady, opens the song; later, Collen cleverly borrows from himself, with rhythm guitar bits that recall 'Armageddon It'. His solo is brazen, aggressive and a bit retro, with embedded octaves and a touch of wah-wah. *This* sounds like Leppard, but updated.

It was the album's second single, hitting a modest number 30 on the US *Billboard* Mainstream Rock chart.

'Torn To Shreds' (Allen/Campbell/Collen/Elliott/Savage)
This tune rocks pretty hard – for this album, anyway – but maintains a mature balance, front to back, with a clean intro and outro sandwiching an intense central theme in which Elliott mashes up remorse, confession and a plea for redemption. The guitar work is less nuanced than usual, but the isolated moments are poignant. The song is melodic enough, but structurally monotonous. Not quite phoned in, but nothing to get excited about.

'Love Don't Lie' (Allen/Campbell/Collen/Elliott/Savage)
This next band composition is a bold sonic experiment: the rhythm guitar shimmers with a 1960s-style vibrato, and the lead solo is played in octaves. Still, the tune is melodic and riff-laden, powerful without being too intense. Elliott again keeps his vocals controlled and focused; it's like he knows his screaming days are over and is in search of his post-Lange voice, and this is one of the songs where he's in that zone.

Again, there's structural monotony, offset by great dynamics and smart production, and the lead solo is little more than a finger exercise – but it works. This is another song that isn't amazing, but it's easy to see Leppard going down this road a little further and finding interesting things.

'Gravity' (Campbell/PJ Smith)
Another tune from the team of Campbell and his Clockmate PJ Smith, this percussive adventure wants to rock out, but is reined in to some corner of pop-funk, where it parades great vocals and riffs, but never really cuts loose. Elliott raps a lot, which is not his forté. The reasoning behind this track's arrangement and production is unclear; do Leppard really need to stretch out onto Prince's turf? Another good song that fell well short of greatness.

'Cry' (Allen/Campbell/Collen/Elliott/Savage)
Probably the album's hardest-rocking, this track is tight and powerful, showing many traces of *Hysteria*-era production while eschewing others. There are octaves in the chorus vocals but no harmonies, a brilliant dynamic drop halfway through, strategic dead-stops and a wailing lead solo. Allen's snare sounds fantastic. But, once again, there's almost no structure to the song at all: most of the song is a drone on A major – common in alternative rock, uncommon for Leppard.

'Girl Like You' (Allen/Campbell/Collen/Elliott/Savage)
As the album starts to wind down, this track comes along – after three in a row that were compositionally uninspired – and restores the Leppard song

machine of old. Verse, bridge and chorus are all in different keys, and the song modulates joyously upward on its final chorus.

This is a boy-girl song, a few steps back thematically on what is otherwise a more mature relationship-oriented album, but it serves up that great Leppard amorè without all that misogyny. Elliott has never been shy about confessing his vulnerability, even at his most outlandishly brash, but this lyric reeks of sincerity.

There's great vocal back-and-forth between Elliott and his ensemble brothers in the chorus, and the guitar work is infectiously riff-heavy, especially when Savage is in sync. They could have done more with it; at 2:51, it's one of three tracks on the album that clock in under three minutes. That kind of brevity is unprecedented for Leppard.

'Let Me Be The One' (Allen/Campbell/Collen/Elliott/Savage)
The album's final ballad is strong, well-crafted, well-produced and another earnest entry in what is now a growing Leppard adult contemporary catalogue. It is smooth, melodic and modulates from verse to chorus in a way that conveys Elliott's lyrical plea for acceptance and emotional intimacy. It throws us back into wondering 'Who is this band, exactly?', but we're gratified that Leppard can write an effective ballad without the co-writers.

'Scar' (Allen/Campbell/Collen/Elliott/Savage/Woodroffe)
The album ends with a punch, a track with an almost *Hysteria*-era feel, with a powerful, riff-driven intro leading into a restrained, ethereal verse over clean guitar. The theme is inconsistent with the rest of the album, serving up bitter recrimination – to which the music is perfectly wed. It's an unexpected treat, another out-of-the-blue moment on an album packed with them, and one of the best tracks to be found here.

UK/Japanese Bonus Tracks
'Kiss The Day' (Allen/Campbell/Collen/Elliott/Savage)
'Long, Long Way To Go' (Acoustic) (Wayne Hector/Steve Robson)

B-Sides
'Love Don't Lie' (Demo)
'Now' (Acoustic)

Yeah! (2006)

Personnel:
Joe Elliott: lead and backing vocals, piano; all instruments on bonus track 'Space Oddity'
Rick Savage: bass, vocals; lead vocals, all instruments on 'Dear Friends'
Phil Collen: lead guitar, vocals; lead vocals on 'Stay With Me'; lead vocals, all instruments on bonus track 'Search And Destroy'
Rick Allen: drums, percussion
Vivian Campbell: lead guitar, vocals
EmmGryner: backing vocals, piano
Ian Hunter: spoken intro on 'The Golden Age Of Rock 'N' Roll'
Justin Hawkins: backing vocals
Marc Danzelsen: drums and backing vocals on bonus track 'American Girl'
John 'Bro' Campbell: saxophone
Ronan McHugh: Mellotron
Anita Thomas-Collen, Kristine Elliott, Stevie Vann-Lange: backing vocals
Recorded at Joe's Garage, Dublin, in the summer of 2004
Producers: Def Leppard, Ronan McHugh
Engineers: Ronan McHugh
Released: 23 May 2006
Label: Mercury, Island
Certification: none
Chart activity: US *Billboard* 200: 16, UK Rock & Metal Albums: 4, UK Albums: 52
Running time: 53:43

It's fair to say Leppard had experienced a touch of schizophrenia in that period between the mid-1990s and mid-2000s, from *Slang* through *X*. They'd been all over the map, boldly experimenting and returning to form and genre-hopping. What next? A cover album, of course. They began revisiting the canons of the artists that had inspired them – T. Rex, David Bowie, Thin Lizzy, Mott the Hoople, Badfinger – and decided to *really* get back to their roots, paying tribute to their heroes.

At face value, this seems both a hare-brained approach to making a comeback and a breathtakingly risky thing to do. They were surely advised by many that this wasn't the best way to go, but it turned out to be just what the band – and their career – needed. *Yeah!* was a shot of pure adrenaline, right when Leppard needed it most.

The idea was primarily Elliott's – a concept he had held in his mind since the *Pyromania* days: 'This has to be a statement about where we came from', he said on the band's website. 'It's like we're gonna do David Essex because we think 'Rock On' is an awesome song. We're gonna do Badfinger. We're gonna do Thin Lizzy. We're gonna do The Faces. We're gonna do T. Rex and Sweet and E.L.O. because these are the songs that led us to where we were.'

The album proper includes 14 cover tunes from the artists above, plus Rod Stewart, Roxy Music and others, and a batch of additional covers that made it onto retail versions of the album as bonus tracks. It's a cornucopia of classic rock celebration for anyone who loves the genre, and Leppard were the band who could not only get away with it but bring it off perfectly.

The band's reverence for the artists they were covering is clear in their refusal to tinker much with the original arrangements; they weren't trying to 're-interpret' those great songs, or 'make them their own', but to simply offer homage. It was further clarified by their choices: with only a couple of exceptions, they didn't choose their idols' best-known works, but deep cuts that they felt deserved the light of day – which they provided, in truckloads. The result was a marvellous achievement, especially in the millennial musical age of emo, pop punk and rap rock: it reminded the fans born of Leppard's own generation what they were really about, surfacing a sound with a forceful and poignant veneer.

Touring with Journey in 2006 after the album's release, Leppard threw in some Bowie and David Essex – indulging in homage to the music of their youth.

The album went to number 16 in the US and number 52 in the UK. *Rolling Stone*'s Andy Greene considered *Yeah!* to be '[Def Leppard's] most convincing album in 14 years', adding that 'It's good enough just to hear the band having fun and to see where all the *Hysteria* came from.'

'They sound live and vigorous', wrote Stephen Thomas Erlewine in *Allmusic*. '*Yeah!* is a sheer delight, a roaring rock 'n' roll record that's their best album since *Hysteria*. Often, cover albums get bogged down in reverence or ambition, as artists either offer interpretations that are straight copies or fussy reinterpretations as they busily try to make a favourite song their own. That's not the case here.'

Cover Art

The cover is as glam as its contents, designed by Vartan, putting the Leppards themselves on its face for the first time (photos by Clay Patrick McBride). There is also a booklet featuring each member of the band recreating a cover of a classic album; legendary photographer Mick Rock shot the band photos inside.

'20th Century Boy' (Marc Bolan)

Released as a single on 21 August 2006
The band come out of the gate strong with this T. Rex chestnut, chosen over the more obvious 'Get It On'. Alternately gritty and celestial, Leppard lay it down faithfully, right down to the soprano backing harmonies. The central riff around which the song is built is all Leppard, and Elliott's vocal easily snares Marc Bolan's precious machismo.

It was the album's third single, and didn't chart.

'Rock On' (David Essex)
Released as a single in May 2006
Charts: US *Billboard* Hard Rock: 18
Unmatched in the classic rock canon for minimalist texture, 'Rock On' is an exemplary entry here. It says a lot about Leppard that this track sits so high on their pedestal; it's a masterful song on many levels, seamlessly integrating an early techno vibe with a swamp-rock atmosphere. Leppard's recent percussion experiments serve the song well, and their dollops of hot guitar enhance the song without distraction.

It was the album's second single, going to number 18 on the US *Billboard* Hard Rock chart. In their 2006 live performances, Leppard segued into this song from Savage's bass solo.

'Hanging On The Telephone' (Jack Lee)
Originally recorded by The Nerves, this Blondie track was the result of another toss-up: Elliott preferred tackling 'One Way Or Another'. But this choice worked out well, a late-1970s monograph that gave Allen and Savage a punk beat they could lay into and a guitar romp for Collen and Campbell. Where Debbie Harry's vocal was seductive, Joe Elliott's sounds like a negotiation, and the result is exhilarating.

'Waterloo Sunset' (Ray Davies)
This Kinks track, very much a product of its time, is a superb choice for Leppard treatment: the original is deliciously melodic, with shifting guitar textures and vocal counterpoint and arresting key changes – all the building blocks of great Leppard.

Elliott succumbs to the temptation to sound like Ray Davies, but he's so good at it that it's hard to mind.

'Hell Raiser' (Mike Chapman/Nicky Chinn)
This is not their first Sweet cover; that band had a huge influence on the Leppards in their boyhoods, and they answer it again with this raucous dive, preserving all the song's sharp edges and glammy preening. Every Leppard's performance shines here; they were clearly having a ball.

'10538 Overture' (Jeff Lynne)
When Leppard set out to do *Yeah!*, they excluded The Beatles, The Stones, Led Zeppelin and Queen from cover eligibility (out of sheer awe, we can safely assume). That makes this ELO choice a Trojan horse of sorts, as writer Jeff Lynne (himself a Beatles worshipper) embedded plenty of Beatle-isms in the song. '10538 Overture' wants to grow up to be 'I Am The Walrus', and its bendy strings, French horns and descending-scale construction are all perfectly preserved in Leppard's rendition, the only standout distinction being that Leppard's version is much tighter and more intense.

'Street Life' (Bryan Ferry)
This over-the-top glamfest is a par for Roxy Music – another group high on Leppard's childhood idols list – and notable for riffs that are very melodic and a vocal melody that isn't. Leppard sets aside the keyboard dissonance of the original version's intro in favour of power guitar, and Elliott gives the lyric all the sass he can. You can almost taste the lipstick.

'Drive-In Saturday' (David Bowie)
With all of Bowie to choose from, this song was a particularly tasteful choice: Bowie may be the god of glam, but the album is already swimming in glam, so why not go full retro? The original Bowie single was heavy doo-wop, and while it went unnoticed in the US, the homeland gave it a number three on the charts. Leppard's take is lovingly rendered, down to Elliott's joyous vocal and a flurry of marvellous saxophone licks. Allen's snare is particularly punchy, the guitars and bass sway respectfully and the nostalgia is intoxicating.

What's great about the track is that the nostalgia is utterly ironic, in a way that only Bowie could manage: the song isn't about the 1950s, but a post-apocalyptic society that can't remember how sex works, and has to learn from old movies – giving 'drive-in Saturday' a whole new meaning. This had to have been greatly appealing to the band; it's just the sort of wink-nudge fun they loved in their youth.

'Little Bit Of Love' (Paul Rodgers/Paul Kossoff/Andy Fraser/Simon Kirke)
This flower-power gem is a nod to the relentless optimism that pervades Leppard's work, a positive upbeat spirit that was the exception rather than the rule in their youth. Free generated many such tunes, and this one is simple and straightforward; Leppard delivers it largely unmodified, though with a little more heat in the guitars.

'The Golden Age Of Rock 'N' Roll' (Ian Hunter)
Leppard's love of anthems is a defining trait, and this one from Mott the Hoople – while not the best one from its era – overflows with the exaltation that Leppard themselves strive for. Not only do they preserve the original track's gospel-ish intro (with Ian Hunter himself delivering the spoken line, 'Ladies and gentlemen – the Golden Age of Rock and Roll!'), but they also preserve the pulsating piano and the over-the-top lead break (though Leppard put more juice into it).

'No Matter What' (Pete Ham)
Released as a single on 16 May 2005
Charts: US *Billboard* Adult Top 40: 24
Badfinger's more modest intensity is well-suited to Leppard; more pop than rock, but plenty of game, like Leppard themselves in 2006. This, their second-biggest hit, translates perfectly: the tight verse rhythm, the expansive chorus vocals and the stops are all faithfully executed, and despite the polish, the

band are clearly loving every second of it. (It's also a swoon towards The Beatles, whose influence on Badfinger was definitive.)

It was the album's first single.

'He's Gonna Step On You Again' (John Kongos/Christos Demetríou)
Not only is this raucous, riff-driven song almost completely unknown to rock fans on the Western side of the pond, but the artist himself is obscure. Kongos is a South African singer-songwriter who never made the US top 40 but played very well in England, and this infectious tune boasts African rhythms that stuck in Leppard's minds when they were writing and recording, for instance, 'Rocket'. (In a historical note, it's also listed in *The Guinness Book Of World Records* as the first song to use a sample; this is technically untrue, as the recording, in fact, incorporates a tape loop.)

Leppard lay back on the exotic rhythm, focusing more on the riffs, though Allen's more straightforward playing is inspired.

'Don't Believe A Word' (Phil Lynott)
There could be no Leppard cover album without a Thin Lizzy song; they were probably Leppard's single greatest inspiration, over and above all their many influences. This one is a great choice, giving Collen and Campbell all the harmony lines they could ever want, and their recreation of the solo break in particular updates the tone and feel of the original track without losing any of its edge. Elliott deftly matches Phil Lynott's soulful vocal delivery.

'Stay With Me' (Rod Stewart/Ronnie Wood)
Phil Collen takes over the microphone on this final track, acquitting himself admirably on this Rod Stewart/Faces classic. His voice has all the grit and self-loathing of the original – you can't pull this song off without it – and the band's harsh sonic edge supports him well. As with all the other tracks, this one maintains fidelity to the original, right down to the Wurlitzer electric piano. It wraps up the album perfectly.

Itunes Bonus Track
'How Does It Feel' (Slade) (Noddy Holder/Jim Lea)
This leftover from the *Yeah!* sessions is a stripped-down version of the 1975 Slade single – piano and vocals. It's a treat, bright and spirited, but lacking the backing tracks that kick in on the original. Elliott's vocal is exceptionally emotive and earnest, and he accompanies himself very capably on the piano. It's arguable that this version tops Slade's.

Target Bonus Tracks
'Action' (Live) (The Sweet) (Brian Connolly/Andy Scott/Steve Priest/Mick Tucker/Benny Gallagher/Graham Lyle)
Recorded during the band's 2005 tour, this live version of The Sweet tune

already covered on *Retro Active* is pure tribute; the band love this tune from their childhood, and fires it off with rowdy, joyous energy.

'When I'm Dead And Gone' (McGuinness Flint) (Benny Gallagher/ Graham Lyle)
Another *Yeah!* leftover, this unlikely choice actually has a lot going for it – a wistful country vibe, well-rendered with just voices and guitars. It lacks the quirky sonic variety of McGuinness Flint's folksy original, but stands up well in this fresh interpretation.

Best Buy Bonus Tracks
'How Does It Feel' (Slade) (Noddy Holder/Jim Lea)
See above.

'No Matter What' (Live) (Badfinger) (Pete Ham)
Also from the 2005 tour, this live version of the Badfinger track, included on *Yeah!*, is delivered with happy garage-band energy, another example of Leppard reliving their beloved British rock boyhood.

'Winter Song' (Lindisfarne) (Alan Hull)
From Lindisfarne's 1970 debut album *Nicely Out Of Tune*, this guitar-and-vocal cover from the *Yeah!* sessions isn't bad at all, but lacks the melancholy that made the original a standout track.

Japanese Bonus Tracks
'American Girl' (Tom Petty)
It's no stretch imagining Leppard choosing this single from Tom Petty's debut album; it's raucous, uninhibited and all about sex. It's a little odd that they turned to America for *Yeah!* material (this one didn't make the cut), but it's in the right time-frame: the track was originally released in the mid-1970s, like much of their cover album's content. Leppard's version is lovingly faithful to the original, with guitar flourishes and rhythmic accents in the instrumental break that actually improve on Petty's version.

'Search And Destroy' (The Stooges) (Iggy Pop/James Williamson)
An Iggy Pop tune certainly wouldn't have been out of place on *Yeah!*. This one, originally released in 1973 by Iggy and the Stooges, has the rowdy energy and rough edges of youth that defined the adolescent Leppards. Their take (which likewise didn't make the cut) is capable, suffering only from the silliness of being put forth by men past 40.

Wal-Mart Bonus EP
'American Girl' (Tom Petty)
See above.

'Search And Destroy' (The Stooges) (Iggy Pop/James Williamson)
See above.

'Space Oddity' (David Bowie)
Leppard had referenced this track in 'Rocket', almost two decades earlier, a nod then (and in this cover) to the glam-rock icon of their early teenage years. This is a marvellous, painstaking recreation: Leppard recreate the tune perfectly, from the low and ominous vocals (with octave echo) of the first verse to the handclaps in the acoustic guitar break to the Mellotron paddings Rick Wakeman laid down on the original. All that's missing is the desperate anxiety and resignation of Bowie's voice, unmistakable on the original, which Elliott can't recapture. Why the track didn't make *Yeah!* is anybody's guess.

'Dear Friends' (Queen) (Brian May)
A sorrowful ballad appearing on Queen's *Sheer Heart Attack* (1974), a seminal album from Leppard's youth, this simple piano-and-vocal track gets the full Leppard treatment, becoming a brief but fast-tempo rocker. This transforms the song from a moment of comfort to a celebratory salute. Interesting but not essential, which is probably why it was dropped from the album. The missed opportunity was to leave the backing sparse and showcase Leppard's exquisite, Queen-like harmony vocals.

'Heartbeat' (Jobriath)
The original incarnation of this track from American glam rocker Jobriath echoes early Elton John – another Leppard influence. The source track is, for the most part, just piano and vocal; the Leppard version arguably improves on it, as Elliott's vocal reading is lush and emotive, with tasteful strings augmenting the piano backing. It was probably too slow and brief to have been suitable for *Yeah!*.

Songs From The Sparkle Lounge (2008)

Personnel:
Joe Elliott: lead and backing vocals
Rick Savage: bass, vocals, guitars
Phil Collen: guitars, vocals
Rick Allen: drums, backing vocals
Vivian Campbell: guitars, vocals
Tim McGraw: vocals on 'Nine Lives'
Recorded at Joe's Garage (Dublin) between 2006 and 2008
Producers: Ronan McHugh, Def Leppard
Engineers: Ronan McHugh, Ger McDonnell, Preston Pope
Released: 25 April 2008
Label: Mercury, Island, Universal Music Enterprises
Certification: none
Chart activity: US *Billboard* 200: 5, US *Billboard* Top Hard Rock Albums: 1, US *Billboard* Top Rock Albums: 1, UK Rock & Metal Albums: 1, UK Albums: 10
Running time: 39:12

Yeah! had revitalised Leppard, restoring their sense of who they were and pumping energy back into their creative process, which had been dormant since *X* (*Yeah!* hadn't required any original writing or arranging). So pent up was this creative energy that they managed to record and release *Songs From The Sparkle Lounge* a mere 23 months after *Yeah!* – the fastest album turnaround since *High 'N' Dry/Pyromania,* a quarter of a century earlier (not counting *Adrenalize/Retro Active,* since the latter wasn't a from-scratch original album). And they did it while touring in between.

Part of this rapid turnaround happened because the songs they brought in for *Sparkle Lounge* were already mostly written before they even began work on the album. The Leppards had been writing individually while on the road: nine of the album's 11 tracks have solo writing credits (two apiece from Elliott, Collen and Savage; three from Campbell). 'We took a lot of songs that were already half-written, and it was a lot easier', Elliott said in an interview on the band's website. 'We'd go in and really work on these songs, and by the time we started recording them, we knew them really well and there was not that much of a learning process. So, it was probably the best recording situation for new music we've ever had.'

Collen wasn't thrilled with the lack of collaboration: 'It was like doing four separate projects, and everybody came in with different songs', he told *Inside Out,* adding that he didn't feel they'd pushed each other 'musically and creatively.'

Mutt Lange had originally been set to return as producer, and he would have insisted on that collaboration (and joined in himself), but conflicting schedules nixed that plan, and Ronan McHugh, who had co-produced *Yeah!*, took point.

The band subsequently decided to 'use 2008 production techniques, if you like, to make it sound more like a 1970s record', Elliott said. 'The whole record's got a 1970s feel. By our standards, it's a very adventurous album.' There was also a conscious inspiration from the AC/DC and Led Zeppelin songs of the band's youth.

'Sparkle Lounge' refers to the tuning trailer used by the band on tour, Elliott told *Billboard.* 'The crew started having a bit of fun with it, putting in sparkly lights, candles, incense – you name it. It turned into this very atmospheric little workspace.'

With a total running time of only 39:12, it is the shortest album of Def Leppard's career. Though the album earned no RIAA or OCC certifications, it charted very well, climbing to number five on the US *Billboard* 200 and number ten on the UK Albums charts – the best US chart performance by a Leppard album since *Adrenalize,* 16 years earlier. It also went to number one on both the US *Billboard* Top Hard Rock Albums and US *Billboard* Top Rock Albums charts, and number one on the UK Rock & Metal Albums chart. Neither of the album's two singles charted in either the US or the UK. No Leppard single, in fact, would chart again in either the US or UK until 2022.

'In the 1990s, when producer Robert 'Mutt' Lange disappeared into Switzerland with Shania Twain and dump trucks full of cash, he left Def Leppard stranded', wrote Andy Greene in *Rolling Stone.* 'Lange produced and co-wrote their best-selling release, *Hysteria,* and the band tries hard to re-create that album's magic on *Songs From The Sparkle Lounge.* 'Go', the opener, has the group's signature layered vocals, crunching guitars and 1970s glam-rock vibe. But when the fivesome team up with Tim McGraw in a desperate country-crossover attempt on 'Nine Lives', the results aren't pretty. From there, the band's on cruise control – especially on the politically tinged 'Cruise Control' and the Kansas-style power ballad 'Love' – with songs that feel like inferior versions of hits two decades past. Def Leppard show signs of life on the headbanging 'Bad Actress', which takes on the Lindsay Lohans of the world, but it's clear they're missing their old producer. We await their 2010 Timbaland-aided comeback.'

'With *Songs From The Sparkle Lounge,* the band try to regain their earlier spirit, but mostly succeed in summoning up polite echoes of former glories, some not even their own', wrote Andy Gill in *The Independent.* 'The strident 'Hallucinate' could be by Bryan Adams, the arpeggiated guitar of 'Gotta Let It Go' recalls '(Don't Fear) The Reaper' and 'Come Undone' opens like some heavy metal alchemist's dream combination of 'Kashmir' and 'Freebird'.'

Other reviews were similarly mixed: 'It's a partially successful successor to *Yeah!,* following through on some of the overall feel and punch but lacking enough songs to truly bring it across the goal line', wrote Stephen Thomas Erlewine in *Allmusic. Sputnikmusic* was slightly more positive: 'What saves this album from being a complete bomb is the fact that nothing on it is a bomb. In fact, none of the songs are bad. They definitely aren't, however, distinguishable, well-crafted and memorable. There is no magical art to them, no gallant hooks that will stay with you for eternity, no rock for the ages here.'

Cover Art

The cover of *Sparkle Lounge,* created by Alias Designs under the direction of Richard Proctor, was inspired by *Sgt. Pepper's Lonely Hearts Club Band:* it includes photos of the band, along with numerous historical figures, friends and family, and record company and management personnel.

'In the summer of 2007, Joe called to say that the new album was almost done and they had a 99% finished title', Proctor said in an interview on the band's website. 'They already had the idea of how they wanted the cover to look: *Sgt. Pepper* meets *Monty Python*, using iconic historical figures to make up the audience, along with pictures of themselves from childhood through to the present day. The first few drafts worked really well, until we considered the copyright issue and image rights. This caused us to re-address this initial idea and a few alternative covers were produced. One of them became the cover for the 'Nine Lives' single and also ended up being used on the inside of the *Sparkle Lounge* booklet. Then, at the last minute, we came a full 360 and went back to the first idea of the audience, but we used pics of family, friends and crew members ... arguably iconic in their own right!'

'Go' (Collen/Elliott)

The band come out heavy on this opening track, the first of the album's two collaborations. An intense guitar riff erupts over a thundering rhythm, and Elliott comes in, sounding angry and aggressive. They haven't sounded like this in a long time, and the song's theatrics are promising. But the track never really develops; there's a monotony to it that's very un-Leppard-like, the entire track pounding out the same rhythm, circling the same Eb-fifth relentlessly, leaving barely any distinction between verse and chorus, let alone the wonderful structures and complexities and surprises we've come to expect.

'Nine Lives' (Collen/Elliott/Tim McGraw/Rick Savage)

Released as a single on 27 April 2008

Country star Tim McGraw co-wrote and sang on this second collaborative track, which was facilitated by Rick Allen's brother, Robert, who happened to be McGraw's tour manager. The justification: a gimmick like McGraw on a Leppard track would possibly get it on the radio. It is certainly radio-worthy, though it didn't manage to chart in either the US or the UK. It's a friendlier, more accessible song than its immediate predecessor, and we can hear more of the Leppard we're used to. The guitar work is spirited and varied, and the bridge harmonies are superb. The chorus isn't quite an anthem, but it's certainly a sing-along.

'C'mon C'mon' (Savage)

Released as a single on 14 July 2008

The album's second single (which was unsuccessful as the first) is nonetheless a breathless riff machine in the best tradition of Leppard – ear-catching and hard-rocking. It's as shallow as a backyard wading pool, but it's impossible not to like it. The band's trademark dynamics are back, with a break in the song where Savage's bass wanders high up his fretboard, the band then crashing back into the song's bridge – the kind of thing that Mutt Lange used to encourage. The tune has some callback to the 1980s, echoing Mötley Crüe a little – but it doesn't do them any harm.

'Love' (Savage)

As this ballad opens, we get the feeling we're back in *X,* doing adult contemporary. There's a soft, gentle acoustic guitar fingerpicked beneath Elliott's quiet and contemplative voice, and the backing vocals are straight off a Carpenters record. But the music heats up at around 1:45, with Allen and Savage kicking in alongside a pair of electric guitars. Those easy-listening vocals persist, Elliott remains pensive, but a very theatrical modulation, emphasised by rolling toms, splashing cymbals and tense orchestral strings, takes us into a screaming lead guitar solo, and suddenly the song is not so much the Carpenters as Queen, which is, of course, by design.

'Tomorrow' (Collen)

Any Phil Collen composition is going to be a riff feast, and this one has them to spare: there are plenty of *Hysteria*-era guitar ornaments, some great melodic stretches for Elliott and Collen's lead solo is borderline-hummable. All of this adds up to a track that's certainly enjoyable but ultimately unremarkable.

'Cruise Control' (Campbell)

This tense, edgy track gets lots of points for its gritty, defiant tone and out-of-the-box innovations, like Savage's steady stream of 16th notes in the bassline and the moody, low-octave notes in the backing vocals. What it's lacking is the hooks of its predecessors.

The lyrics, which focus disturbingly on religious mania, suggest that this is the rare 'message' tune from Leppard – and that this element took precedence over user-friendliness.

'Hallucinate' (Collen)

The riffs are back and plentiful in another Collen tune that restores the Leppard guitar dynamic of old: he and Campbell pitch and catch gleefully alongside Elliott's matter-of-fact delivery. Collen's lead is blazing fun, but again, the track is well shy of being anything great.

'Only The Good Die Young' (Campbell)

If you're going to lift song titles off Billy Joel's stuff, you'd better deliver a winner. This song really wants to be, with its catchy chorus and reminiscent theme; the 'Strawberry Fields Forever' Mellotron on the verse is a nice touch. There's even an old-school organ part in there, and Campbell's lead solo is pure fun. It's a decent track, but Billy Joel can sleep comfortably.

'Bad Actress' (Elliott)

Elliott's glam roots are showing in this send-up of celebrity culture. The music, sharp and biting, reflects the cynical traps of pop stardom, but this kind of commentary really isn't Leppard's thing. Even so, Allen and Savage infuse the track with runaway energy that in turn kicks both Collen and Campbell up a notch.

'Come Undone' (Elliott)

Elliott's second contribution is an album highlight, and it's a shame it's hidden in the back. It's yet another song of desperation, with Elliott once again at some woman's mercy, but he does those so well we don't mind. The track is tight, intense, riff-laden and coloured in vintage Leppard touches – fantastic chorus harmonies, mid-song gear shifts – and some not-so-standard treats, like slide and wah-wah guitar.

'Gotta Let It Go' (Campbell)

The album closes out with this retro-feeling mood piece that wants to combine the early 1970s Hollies with Blue Öyster Cult. The guitar work here might seem derivative, but it's likely a homage; Leppard have long offered musical tribute to their boyhood heroes, and why shouldn't Campbell, who wrote the track, have a turn?

There's a very Lange-esque bridge with ear-grabbing chords, and an intense chorus with heavy guitar and reliable harmonies – but Campbell's thing seems to be in the lyrics, where he's pontificating on futility and empty pursuits. He really is a talented writer, with more apparent thematic range than his peers, and it's good that he had three tracks to himself this time out.

Uk And iTunes Bonus Track

'Love' (Piano Version)

Japanese Bonus Tracks

'Love' (Piano Version)
'Nine Lives' (w/out Tim McGraw)

Def Leppard (2015)

Personnel:
Joe Elliott: lead and backing vocals, acoustic guitar
Rick Savage: bass, guitars, lead and backing vocals
Phil Collen: guitars, lead and backing vocals
Rick Allen: drums, percussion, lead vocals
Vivian Campbell: guitars, lead and backing vocals
Ronan McHugh: keyboards, Mellotron, bouzouki
Debbi Blackwell-Cook: backing vocals
Recorded at Joe's Garage (Dublin) and Phil's Sweat Shop (California) between 2006 and 2008
Producers: Ronan McHugh, Def Leppard
Engineer: Ronan McHugh
Released: 30 October 2015
Label: Bludgeon Riffola/Mailboat (US); earMUSIC (Europe)
Certification: none
Chart activity: US *Billboard* 200: 10, US *Billboard* Top Rock Albums: 1, US *Billboard* Top Hard Rock Albums: 1, UK Albums: 11, UK Rock & Metal Albums: 1
Running time: 52:39

Long-time fans had been spoiled, getting four albums in nine years between *Euphoria* and *Sparkle Lounge;* not since the 1980s had Leppard been that prolific. But after the latter, they were back to their old ways, letting many years pass between albums. They took their sweet time getting around to this one, though they did put out the excellent *Mirror Ball – Live & More* set, featuring songs spanning their entire career alongside three new studio tracks, including the textbook 'Undefeated'.

The truth is that it simply didn't matter anymore. The music industry had changed so much in the 35-plus years since Leppard had started that any worries about the band's identity were now pointless; the market no longer required new albums to tour on or radio singles. Making peace with their irrelevance, the band were now free to simply have fun, go on parading for their die-hard fanbase and abandon quests for reinvention or comparisons to their earlier selves.

That's the thinking behind the title of this album; when they finally got around to making it, they realised they could just be who they were, write what they pleased and not worry about callbacks to any particular period in their journey. What's more, they were writing together again; of the album's 14 tracks, all but five were co-written, rather than solo compositions. Phil Collen called it 'the most diverse thing we've ever done' and rated it their best album since *Hysteria*.

Another caution-to-the-wind step was the recording of a song – 'We Belong' – on which all five members sang lead, even Rick Allen. 'It was something I was quite insistent we do, just because people always talk about how great the BVs are in this band', Elliott told *Rolling Stone*. 'So, I thought, 'Well, wouldn't it be nice to have every guy sing separately, and let people hear how good the voices are *au naturel*?' We were just taking advantage of the fact that everybody in this band can sing, just like everyone in The Beatles could sing – even Ringo! Once we coaxed Rick Allen into doing the first line of the second verse, we were off. We knew it was gonna be a good one.'

This new freedom had the odd effect of garnering the very accolades they no longer cared about; the album had the *Billboard* top ten in the US and the top 20 in the UK, and went to number one on the *Billboard* Top Rock Albums, Top Hard Rock Albums and Independent Albums charts.

'There's something subtly different about *Def Leppard,* compared to other recent Def Leppard albums', according to *Deciblerogue's* review. 'Could it be something as simple as Def Leppard being allowed to be Def Leppard again? After all, this is the first album they've ever recorded with no record deal in place. Whatever the reason, *Def Leppard* has been more than worth the wait. Sure, I've been a fan of the band for much of my life, so I may be slightly biased in my opinion. However, over the years, I've been waiting for a Def Leppard album which could hold a candle to *Hysteria*. It's here.'

'It is all things Def Leppard, with no apologies for what and who they are', per *The Prog Report*. 'After decades of churning out hits, it remains that no one sounds like this band and that is why they still fill arenas to this day. This album is a celebration of the band and one that fans will love and blast out loud.'

Drew's Reviews was more positive still: 'Not a junker in the whole lot and anyone could benefit from the live treatment. Does it measure up to the iconic *Hysteria* or *Pyromania*? Nothing ever will, which seems to be the point. Each album stands on its own.'

'Fans can get excited though, no matter what era of the band you favor,' according to *Melodirock,* 'because at the heart of it, this is the most authentic Def Leppard album in two decades and features a monster production and beautiful mix, where harmonies and guitars rule the day, but the rhythm section and vocalist Joe Elliott are all equally showcased.'

Cover Art

After the gaudy exercise of *Sparkle Lounge,* it surely felt right to the band to wrap a return-to-form album in a return-to-form cover. Def Leppard's art was as straightforward as could be: the classic angular Leppard logo breaking through glass, shards flying everywhere, designed and executed by Richard Smith Illustration.

'Let's Go' (Savage/Elliott)
Released as a single on 15 September 2015
Kicking off with spacey sound effects reminiscent of *Hysteria,* this opening track (and the album's first single) is 'a call to arms, you know?' according to

Elliott. He told *Rolling Stone* that the song was mostly Savage's work; he just filled in the verse lyrics. 'We knew it was a classic Def Leppard song. It's that three-minute pop-rock stuff with big crunchy guitars and a big chorus,' he said, 'and it has that swaggering, mid-tempo rhythm, like 'Sugar' and 'Rock Of Ages'. The idea was that we wanted something familiar.'

Familiar it is, invoking the feel of Leppard more solidly than anything put forth since the 1990s. After three experimental albums, Leppard announced with this track that they were finally comfortable just being Leppard. 'With its crackling guitar and nuclear-detonation bottom end,' said a review in *Classic Rock,* "Let's Go' doesn't so much revisit 'Pour Some Sugar On Me' as move into its spare room, steal its cornflakes and start sleeping with its wife.'

'Dangerous' (Collen/Elliott)
Released as a single on 12 February 2016
Mostly a Collen track, this second cut (and second single) is straight ahead and unwavering, retaining a four-on-the-floor rhythm without a lot of variation. The guitars have a retro tone, but in the chorus, there's a *Hysteria* feel to the melodic figures filling in around Elliott's earnest delivery. Collen's solo is made up of a wah-wah tone under a clear, vibrato-laden hook. Maybe it's Allen's drumming inspiring him; he sounds like he's once again the exuberant kid who joined the band at 15.

'Man Enough' (Collen/Elliott)
Released as a single on 4 April 2016
If Leppard are ripping themselves off in the opening track, they are surely ripping Queen off in this one. Sav's bass riff is deeply reminiscent of 'Another One Bites The Dust', so much so that *Classic Rock's* review declares 'it should come with its own stick-on handlebar moustaches.' The homage continues with the frequent stops and relatively sparse guitars. It's brilliantly effective; Sav's bass riff (which was actually suggested by Collen, the song's primary writer) is decidedly busier than John Deacon's, but just as infectious and friendly. Allen's drums are tight and focused, and the guitars are disciplined, yet inventive. The track seems written for a long-gone dance floor era, but it is an engaging listen all the same. It was a great choice for a single.

'We Belong' (Elliott)
Released as a single on 8 December 2016
Here's the track mentioned above, the ballad that features all five Leppards contributing a bit of lead vocal. As Leppard ballads go, it's less overwrought than many of its predecessors, laid out earnestly and confidently. The chorus is catchy and warm, and Elliott's lyrics are upbeat and affirming, his delivery leaning (for once) into less-is-more. The use of the other voices really doesn't affect the song much; it seems gimmicky. Still, we almost never hear the other Leppard voices standing alone, so it's kind of a nice moment anyway.

It was the album's final single, but 'Broke 'N' Brokenhearted' might have been a better choice.

'Invincible' (Allen/Elliott)

A rare nod to the punk of their youth, this tune opens with a trebly barrage of 16th-note sameness from Sav, with a sharp snapping snare beneath, evoking The Clash. Featuring a rare songwriting contribution from Allen, the tune is refreshing in that it sounds different from all the other tracks. Elliott practically whispers the song, staying as low-key as possible, an interesting and effective choice as he lays down a lyric about resilience.

'Sea Of Love' (Collen)

Now they open things up completely with this huge-sounding song by Collen. With its bombastic guitars and in-your-face riffs – to say nothing of the soaring choir of voices in the intro (featuring Debbi Blackwell-Cook of Delta Deep) – it's a headlong dive into rock-driven soul. Allen's drums have the jazzy feel of Bill Bruford as Sav's basslines respond in kind.

'Energized' (Collen)

Collen is on a songwriting roll at this point, bringing in yet another completely different kind of tune. This heady ballad is emotionally nuanced, eschewing (as 'We Belong' did) the Leppard ballad formula, shedding modulations and layered guitars. There are, however, some really great harmonies and emotive dynamics reminiscent of the Lange era.

'All Time High' (Elliott)

This track is a little inexplicable, having a palpable 1970s feel, with more than a few clichés and desperation rhymes. I'm not sure what Elliott was thinking when he wrote it, but props for yet another song with a very positive, uplifting feel, even if the song itself is nothing great.

'Battle Of My Own' (Savage/Elliott)

If 'All Time High' is mere filler, this tune is very much the opposite – bold, experimental and mould-shattering. A moody acoustic piece that reads like it wants to be on a *Young Guns* soundtrack, it's guitar-only under Elliott's frenetic vocal for most of the tune, with bass and drums and hot guitars suddenly erupting two-thirds of the way through. It's a masterpiece of tension and dread, with threads of resilience and determination running through it.

'Broke 'N' Brokenhearted' (Collen/Elliott)

It wouldn't be a return-to-form Leppard album without a song about heartbreak – nobody does heartbreak like Leppard! – but this one swings wildly away from its predecessors. While most were spooky ballads, this one is a straight-ahead rocker, packed with energy and power-chord attitude. The narrative is the same old she-done-me-wrong vitriol, but couched in such ludicrous terms that it can't help but come across as playful, which the music underscores. The wordplay is goofy, but in a fun, McCartney-esque way.

'Forever Young' (Collen/Elliott)
Another Collen/Elliott team effort, this track has many classic Leppard earmarks – creative modulations, some strong twin guitar work, rich harmony – and serves up a new take on an old theme. It's a sort of advice piece, addressing unfulfilled longing, and for once, the longing isn't Elliott's.

'Last Dance' (Savage)
This emotive ballad, a moment-of-truth song about a relationship at a crossroads, manages to channel The Eagles with its strong acoustic guitar and smooth harmonies. Percussive fills keep the pace until the rhythm and power guitars kick in, and the song manages to maintain a wistful yet desperate feel as Elliott makes his plea. It's another song that belongs in another time – but it's really refreshing to hear a tune like this on a Leppard album.

'Wings Of An Angel' (Collen/Campbell/Savage/Elliott)
The first group writing collaboration on the album (everyone but Allen contributed), this tune is filled with Leppard-isms, with strong dynamic variation and rhythmic change-ups, strong chorus harmonies and tasty modulations. The verses have a kind of country-music feel to them, the kind Bon Jovi sometimes invoke. Campbell's guitar work shines.

'Blind Faith' (Collen/Campbell/Savage/Elliott)
A trembling guitar riff opens the album's closer, an unexpectedly stylish ballad that serves up an Elliott plea for understanding and resolution, voiced with an interesting mix of confusion and earnestness. The chorus features keyboard strings and a bit of a Beatles style that grows stronger as the song unfolds – quarter-note pulses and bending notes from the strings a la 'I Am The Walrus' – until they go full Leppard in the song's final minute, having paid their luscious tribute. The song wraps with a powerful jam and a blast of rare falsetto from Elliott.

Classic Rock Limited Edition
'We Belong' (Alternate Take)
'Let's Go' (Radio Edit)

Japanese Bonus Tracks
'Last Dance' (Demo)

Diamond Star Halos (2022)

Personnel:
Joe Elliott: lead and backing vocals, guitars, drum machine programming
Rick Savage: bass, guitars, backing vocals
Phil Collen: guitars, backing vocals
Rick Allen: drums
Vivian Campbell: guitars, backing vocals
Alison Krauss: lead vocals on 'This Guitar', 'Lifeless'
Debbi Blackwell-Cooke: backing vocals
Dave Bassett: backing vocals
Mike Garson: piano
Recorded at Joe's Garage (Dublin), Phil's Sweat Shop (California), Sav's Base (Sheffield, UK), Viv's Guitar Shed (New Hampshire) and Ro's Garage (Dublin) between 2020 and 2021
Producers: Ronan McHugh, Def Leppard
Engineers: Ronan McHugh, Ross Hogarth, Joe LaPorta, Def Leppard
Released: 27 May 2022
Label: Bludgeon Riffola, Mercury
Certification: none
Chart activity: US *Billboard* 200: 10, US *Billboard* Top Rock Albums: 2, UK Albums: 5, UK Rock & Metal Albums: 1
Running time: 61:27

On 29 March 2019, Def Leppard were inducted into the Rock and Roll Hall of Fame – more than 40 years after they'd first played together in Sheffield. Queen's Brian May, a huge fan and friend of the band, insisted on inducting them. 'Not everyone realises that these guys are not just crowd pleasers', he said in his introduction. 'They also embody such an amazing technical excellence. They have it all. I regard all these guys as great friends and kind of part of my family; that's why it's so important for me to be here. I wouldn't let anyone else do this.' Underscoring that closeness, May pointed out that Steve Clark and Freddie Mercury had both been lost in the same year. Leppard closed out the Hall of Fame ceremony with a four-song set that included 'Hysteria', 'Rock Of Ages', 'Photograph' and 'Pour Some Sugar On Me'.

For the first time ever, between *Sparkle Lounge* and *Def Leppard,* the band had allowed seven years to pass between albums – but then they immediately turned around and did it *Again.* Before that, they'd managed four studio albums in nine years, from *Euphoria* and *Sparkle Lounge* – but then produced only two in the 14 following years. Even so, the eponymous *Def Leppard* had truly been worth a seven-year wait. *Diamond Star Halos,* perhaps even more so.

There are a couple of ways to characterise *Halos*; on the one hand, it's their COVID album, recorded during the coronavirus quarantine period of 2020-2021; on the other, it's an overt tribute to their glam rock roots, one that integrates their own contribution to that sub-genre. Even so, it stays in the present through the inclusion of country artist Alison Krauss – whose classic rock bona fides have been firmly established through her collaborations with Zep frontman Robert Plant.

The band had been primed to tour with Mötley Crüe, Poison and Joan Jett in the summer of 2020 when everything shut down. Sequestered along with the rest of the planet, it made sense to make good use of the downtime – do a new album. They did this from a variety of locales, each recording wherever they happened to be hunkered down and passing their work over to producer Ronan McHugh in Dublin. Collen, Campbell and Allen were all in the US through this period; Elliott weighed in from Ireland and Savage from the UK. In creating their parts, the band members served largely as their own engineers. 'It really wasn't as complicated or as difficult as it sounds', Collen said in a *Guitar World* interview at the time. 'We've made lots of records without us being in the same room at the same time.'

The album was completed in tandem with the summer 2022 launch of the delayed tour. 'The time off led to an opportunity for us to make a great album,' Campbell summarised in the same *Guitar World* interview, 'so now we're in a position to do a huge tour with a fantastic record to go with it.'

As for the glam rock nod, the title 'Diamond Star Halos' itself derives from T. Rex's 'Get It On', glam's quintessential anthem. Adding some glam cred, the band had Bowie keyboardist Mike Garson sit in on two tracks.

Krauss's participation, which lifts the album above the level of mere nostalgia (albeit first-rate nostalgia), came about when Leppard's manager approached Krauss's manager, asking if she would be interested in singing either 'This Guitar' or 'Lifeless'. According to Collen, 'She listened to them and said, 'I love them both. Can I do both of them?"

With this fourth appearance in the producer's chair, Ronan McHugh – who first worked with Leppard as the engineer of *Euphoria,* more than 20 years earlier – surpassed Mutt Lange in production turns.

At a running time of 61:27, the album is second only to *Hysteria* (62:32) in length in the Leppard canon.

Its chart performance was similar to that of its immediate predecessor – a bit weaker in the US, a bit stronger in the UK. It reached number ten on the US *Billboard* 200, number two on the US *Billboard* Top Rock Albums chart, number five on the UK Albums chart and number one on the UK Rock & Metal Albums chart.

Ultimate Classic Rock was quick to note Leppard's return to form: 'Def Leppard's most obvious callback to glam's glory days as well as their own past triumphs. By pulling inspiration from the genre's heavyweights – David Bowie, Mott the Hoople and T. Rex, whose immortal 'Bang A Gong (Get It On)' gives the LP its title – and sending it through a turn of their career highlights (*Pyromania, Hysteria*), Def Leppard have effectively made a tribute record to themselves featuring 15 new and original songs.' Neil Jeffries of

Classic Rock felt the same. 'It's a lot to absorb, but it's comfortably the best album by this lineup.'

'If *Diamond Star Halos* is a throwback, it's to the golden age of the CD, an era when Leppard thrived delivering albums that pushed the running length of a compact disc', wrote Stephen Thomas Erlewine in *Allmusic*. 'The cumulative effect is almost overwhelming, especially as Def Leppard give it their all in each cut. Leppard crank up the hooks, melodies and amplifiers, adding little bits of distinctive flair along the way ... Taken as a series of moments, the album is pretty compelling – so compelling, in fact, that when they're assembled together, they are almost too much to take in one setting.'

Cover Art

The complex and cryptic cover of *Diamond Star Halos* combines history and mystery, framed in tarot card-style artwork. The image is black and white, with a yellow Leppard logo atop. There's a central eye, around which can be found symbols and objects from Leppard's previous works. 'Essentially, we wanted to have a central theme, so we obviously went with the eye, but we wanted to fill it around with other things from our history, from our other albums', Phil Collen explained. Those 'other things' include the target from the *Pyromania* cover, the diver from the *High 'N' Dry* cover and so on. The artwork is primarily the work of Oliver and Joshua Munden, with contributions from Anton Corbjin and Maryam Malakpour.

'Take What You Want' (Elliott/Savage)
Released as a single on 20 April 2022
The album opens big, with a deceptively poppy intro that features a clean, picked guitar over huge, reverberating power chords. It's a full 45 seconds before the song itself kicks into gear, with a hard rock riff that stands with Leppard's best. It's a turn-it-up moment, one that tells the long-time faithful that Leppard are definitely back – and one that will have even the most casual fan rapidly headbanging.

This is *Hysteria*-quality material showcasing ferocious hooks, lockstep harmonies and powerful rhythms. Elliott is in fine form, belting it out from the soles of his feet, and those classic Leppard dynamics give the song a marvellous bump when that poppy intro cycles back seamlessly after the second chorus. Suddenly, it's a bridge, and Elliott's dynamic shift is craftsmanlike, emoting even more by dialling down the intensity till he sounds almost delicate. Then, Campbell roars back with a sledgehammer lead, which gets the pulse racing.

It was the album's second single.

'Kick' (Dave Bassett/Phil Collen)
Released as a single on 17 March 2022
This anthem, co-written by Colleen and writer/producer Dave Bassett, is arena-ready, complete with sing-along 'na-na-na-na' in its chorus. It's also built

for hand-clapping. It was last-minute; the album was considered finished when Collen brought this one in. It wound up being the third single.

Collen goes full glam on the lead break, squeaking, glissing and hammering like he's 14 again, and when everything but the drums drops out on the penultimate chorus, it's everybody-on-the-feet time. With the possible exception of 'C'mon C'mon', it's hands-down the best anthem the band have come up with since the 1980s.

'Fire It Up' (Collen/Sam Hollander)
Released as a single on 20 May 2022

Yet another power rocker with classic Leppard accoutrement rolls out next (and was the lead-off single). 'Fire It Up' has the earthy scent of Argent, another of the band's boyhood heroes, and it's as sing-along as 'Kick'. The verses are practically a rap; Elliott's delivery is almost untrackable, but the point may be to emphasise the simplicity of the chorus ('Fire it up! Fire it up!'), which is a straight-up chant. The guitars pull off much the same trick, with machine-gun bursts of riff between chorus and verse, followed by a lead break by Collen that opens with lazy half-notes. Allen has found his toms again, stitching together the open spaces and the rat-tat-tat with boomy abandon. Like the previous two tracks, it's a bright neon calling card.

'This Guitar' (CJ Vanston, Elliott) – Alison Krauss

This trippy ballad comes out of nowhere, an almost jarring change in tone from the three previous songs. Pop-country veteran Alison Krauss duets with Elliott, a move made trendy by Robert Plant, and the result is joyous.

The tune is a celebration of music itself, in the tradition of Leppard's US counterparts Boston, but more personal: the duo are singing about how a guitar is ultimately a musician's best friend and most intimate companion. It sounds goofy on its face, but they totally sell it. Better still, the band infuse it with musical nostalgia, as Collen and Campbell sound like a cross between The Eagles and Dr. Hook, clean and unobtrusive. (Savage joins in on 12-string acoustic.)

Overall, it's a completely legitimate country crossover gem, which speaks to Leppard's easy immersion in the music itself. They commit to it totally.

'Sos Emergency' (Elliott/Collen)

And they're back to glamming it up with this animated rocker that sounds like the Leppard of old, characterised by back-and-forth guitar work, big harmonies and an urgent rhythm. It's playful and self-deprecating, a sign that, despite their deep reinvestment in themselves, they aren't taking it all too seriously.

'Liquid Dust' (Collen)

This Collen track features marvellous guitar work that recalls his best days with Steve Clark, when they would layer their parts together and hand off the lead – a style that Clark himself pioneered, respecting the work of earlier guitarists of the New Wave of British Heavy Metal (Priest's Tipton and Downing; Iron Maiden's Smith and Murray). Elliott adds to the moody layers by singing in a lower octave. Indian-sounding keyboard strings emerge in the second verse, adding to the heady atmosphere of a psychedelic Beatles homage that seems to be about reincarnation – 'liquid dust' is us, human beings.

'U Rok Mi' (Collen)

Another track written solely by Collen, this time invoking purely acoustic instruments in a kind of avant-garde folk fashion, going electric with the arrival of its anthemic chorus. It's an irresistible song from top to bottom, but its most welcome feature is the solo-swapping: Collen takes the first one, Campbell the second, then it's back to Collen before they sign off in Thin Lizzy-style harmony.

'Goodbye For Good This Time' (Elliott)

Once we get past this song's title, which sounds like something a 15-year-old boyfriend would shout at a 15-year-old girl who just dumped him, we are treated to a wistful reflection by Elliott (who wrote it), one that wraps frustration and futility in melancholy resolution.

The music beneath his words offers no trace of his bandmates; it's all lonely piano and lush strings (rendered by David Bowie keyboardist Mike Garson) until the chorus, when Allen comes in strong. A bridge later, a Spanish guitar solo ties the tune to its impassioned coda. Like 'This Guitar', it sounds nothing at all like Def Leppard – but it works, largely due to Garson's innovative piano work.

'All We Need' (Elliott/Collen)

This amiable mid-tempo track actually echoes U2 with its elusive, in-the-background guitars, largely monotone measures of bass and popping snare. It might not feel terribly consequential with its routine pop structure and unvarying parts; on the other hand, the lyric is a simple back-to-basics relationship statement by Elliott, and the music firmly supports that idea. The lead break, however, is pure Leppard as we are treated to a seamless key change from A to Bb and a bright, out-front melodic run by Collen. The outro mirrors the intro, drifting back into a U2 haze.

'Open Your Eyes' (Elliott/Collen)

Savage kicks this track open with a busy lick that recalls The Knack, and at first glance, it's a straight-ahead, up-tempo rocker; when Elliott starts to sing, however, he's in half-time – and his voice has a dreamy echo to it. Elliott's lyric is a plea for down-to-earth candour, suggesting that the urgency and cacophony of the rhythm represent the distraction he's eschewing.

If the song is a hymn of awareness, that theme is augmented by the growing unity and power of the harmonies in the bridge. When Sav's bass riff resurfaces before the lead break – a stratospheric sonic wash by Collen – the effect is that Elliott's message is ensnared in struggle, and Collen's emphatic outro lead is a lifeline. It's an almost experimental mashing-up of musical and lyrical themes that earns points for its sonic audacity.

'Gimme A Kiss That Rocks' (Elliott/Collen)
This echo of 'Animal' is an infectious intersection of 1970s glam and Leppard's own history, riff-ridden and exuberant. It's teenager-superficial – a little ludicrous when we remember that these guys are all past 60 – but it's pure fun, and features great lead work by both Collen and Campbell.

'Angels (Can't Help You Now)' (Elliott)
Mike Garson is back on this sad, reflective ballad, laying down piano and atmospheric keyboard pads for a plaintive Elliott vocal about desperation and loss. The harmonies are some of the album's best. Collen's solo is majestic.

'Lifeless' (Elliott/Collen) – Alison Krauss
Alison Krauss returns for this pop country track, blending perfectly with Elliott as the band lay back into an effortless mid-tempo groove that perfectly suits the tune's sorrowful theme. The Leppard-isms are there, however, in the chord changes in the middle of the track and in the decorative guitar licks. Campbell's stylish, melodic lead guitar infuses the song with an undeniable positive vibe that makes it a feel-good song in spite of itself.

'Unbreakable' (Elliott)
The album doesn't really need another heartbreak song, but this track at least has a tight, intense groove far afield of the band's historical mopey wails. The structure of the tune gives it a *Hysteria* feel, surging with riffs and surprising chords – including an ear-pleasing shift from D major to E major in the chorus – that keep the ear alert. The emotional and potent lead solo, again by Campbell, is a stand-out in a song filled with standouts.

'From Here To Eternity' (Savage)
The album ends on a high note with something Leppard hadn't done in ages – an epic. This is Savage going where Elliott usually dwells, in the throes of romantic despair, but this new take has the virtue of almost cinematic, over-the-top melodrama. It couldn't be darker or more depressing, as bleak as the band have ever been.

What really makes it great is the music over which these overwrought sentiments are surfing: the central minor-key rhythm guitar does an arpeggio that unapologetically mimics The Beatles' 'I Want You (She's So Heavy)' as the lead guitar does an octave moan. Fittingly, both Campbell and Collen throw down histrionic solos that surge with edgy energy.

The song goes full Queen in the bridge, into operatic chord progressions and perfect vocal stacks, entrenching the ultra-glam vibe Savage is going for – just the sort of thing that will urge us to let them get away with it.

Deluxe Edition

'Goodbye For Good This Time' (Avant-Garde Mix)
'Lifeless' (Elliott)

Japanese Standard Edition

'Angels (Can't Help You Now)' (Stripped Version)
'This Guitar' (Elliott)

Live Albums

Leppard's live shows have always been stand-up-and-shout, festival-level events, and they remain so more than 40 years on. There are several live documents out there that capture this insatiable energy.

Mirror Ball – Live & More (2011)

Live tracks recorded at venues on the Sparkle Lounge Tour (2008-2009)
Studio tracks recorded at Joe's Garage (Dublin), Phil's Sweat Shop (California), Rick's Place (California, USA) (2009-2011)
Producers: Ronan McHugh, Def Leppard
Engineer: Ronan McHugh
Released: 3 June 2011
Label: Bludgeon Riffola/Mailboat, Frontiers
Certification: Gold (US)
Chart activity: US *Billboard* 200: 16, UK Albums: 44, UK Rock & Metal Albums: 3
Running time: 119:16
Tracklisting: Disc One: 'Rock! Rock! (Till You Drop)', 'Rocket", 'Animal', 'C'mon C'mon', 'Make Love Like A Man', 'Too Late For Love', 'Foolin", 'Nine Lives', 'Love Bites', 'Rock On'
Disc Two: 'Two Steps Behind', 'Bringin' On The Heartbreak', 'Hysteria', 'Armageddon It', 'Photograph', 'Pour Some Sugar On Me', 'Rock Of Ages', 'Let's Get Rocked', 'Action', 'Bad Actress', 'Undefeated' (Elliott; New Studio Track), 'Kings Of The World' (Savage; New Studio Track), 'It's All About Believin" (Collen, Jeffrey Lynn Vanston; New Studio Track)

The band's first standalone live album, recorded during the *Sparkle Lounge Tour*, included cuts from all across their career, as well as three new studio tracks (see below). It included a DVD containing concert and backstage footage.

'Undefeated' (Elliott)

Released as a single on 12 April 2011
Charts: US *Billboard* Heritage Rock: 26
It had been years since Leppard had launched a new anthem, and this one – written by Elliott – came across nicely, encapsulated in the classic Leppard style and exuding an upbeat, triumphant feel. Built for the arena, it fused a heavy, foot-stomping beat with vintage Leppard layered vocals, and took its place on the set lists of the *Rock Of Ages* tour and *Viva! Hysteria* show.

'Kings Of The World' (Savage)

Written by Sav, this exceptional power ballad evokes the music of ELO (and, by extension, The Beatles) – a powerful, compelling composition, executed brilliantly by the band. The lyrics have an introspective, determined 'My Way' theme, which Elliott conveys with sincerity, and the band play the tune with restrained power, holding back just enough to let the vocals take precedence.

Collen's solo leans into Elliott's emotion, conveying the song's quiet sense of satisfaction and appreciation.

'It's All About Believin'' (Collen/C.J. Vanston)

A Collen track co-written with Spinal Tap keyboardist C.J. Vanston, this tune recaptures the guitar sound of the *Hysteria* era, as well as its bright, optimistic tone. The chorus is exuberant, surging with the band's signature harmonies and the sense of hopeful yearning that Elliott does so well. Collen delivers the lead solo on this track, handing in a warm, understated statement that soars in its conclusion.

Viva! Hysteria (2013)

Recorded at The Joint, Las Vegas, between 29 and 30 March, 2013
Producer: Ronan McHugh
Engineer: Ronan McHugh
Released: 22 October 2013
Label: Bludgeon Riffola, Frontiers
Certification: none
Chart activity: US *Billboard* 200: 24, UK Albums: 73, UK Rock & Metal Albums: 6
Running time: 142:42
Tracklisting: Disc One: 'Women', 'Rocket', 'Animal', 'Love Bites', 'Pour Some Sugar On Me', 'Armageddon It', 'Gods Of War', 'Don't Shoot Shotgun', 'Run Riot', 'Hysteria', 'Excitable', 'Love And Affection', 'Rock Of Ages', 'Photograph'
Disc Two: 'Good Morning Freedom', 'Wasted', 'Stagefright', 'Mirror, Mirror (Look Into My Eyes)', 'Action', 'Rock Brigade', 'Undefeated', 'Promises', 'On Through The Night', 'Slang', 'Let It Go', 'Another Hit And Run', 'High 'N' Dry (Saturday Night)', 'Bringin' On The Heartbreak', 'Switch 625'
Japanese Bonus Tracks: 'Acoustic Medley' ('Where Does Love Go When It Dies'/'Now'/'When Love & Hate Collide'/'Have You Ever Needed Someone So Bad'/'Two Steps Behind')
This double-live album, capturing all 12 *Hysteria* tracks and 17 others, was recorded during Leppard's 2013 Las Vegas residency. The *Hysteria* album was performed in its vinyl sequence, front to back.

And There Will Be A Next Time ... Live From Detroit (2017)

Recorded at the DTE Energy Music Theatre on 15 July 2016
Producers: Ronan McHugh, Def Leppard
Engineer: Ronan McHugh
Released: 10 February 2017
Label: Eagle Rock Entertainment
Certification: none
Running time: 112:00
Tracklisting: Disc One: 'Let's Go', 'Animal', 'Let It Go', 'Dangerous', 'Foolin'', 'Love Bites', 'Armageddon It', 'Rock On', 'Man Enough'

Disc Two: 'Rocket', 'Bringin' On The Heartbreak', 'Switch 625', 'Hysteria', 'Let's Get Rocked', 'Pour Some Sugar On Me', 'Rock Of Ages', 'Photograph'

This live show from the band's 2016 tour included tracks from the just-released *Def Leppard* album and a generous assortment of past hits, reaching back to *High 'N' Dry*. The album received restrained praise from critics, praising the band's consistent showmanship but noting that Elliott struggles a bit vocally.

Compilations

The Leppard canon is voluminous at this point, covering decades. The band's best work has been bundled in several collections, capturing a range of musical eras.

Retro Active (1993)

(see above)

Vault: Def Leppard Greatest Hits (1980-1995)

North American tracklisting: 'Pour Some Sugar On Me' (Historia Video Edit), 'Photograph', 'Love Bites', 'Let's Get Rocked', 'Two Steps Behind' (Acoustic Version), 'Animal', 'Foolin'', 'Rocket' (Visualize Video Edit), 'When Love & Hate Collide', 'Armageddon It', 'Have You Ever Needed Someone So Bad', 'Rock Of Ages', 'Photograph', 'Miss You In A Heartbeat' (Acoustic Version), 'Bringin' On The Heartbreak'

European tracklisting: 'Pour Some Sugar On Me' (Historia Video Edit), 'Photograph', 'Love Bites', 'Let's Get Rocked', 'Two Steps Behind' (Acoustic Version), 'Animal', 'Heaven Is', 'Rocket' (Visualize Video Edit), 'When Love & Hate Collide', 'Action', 'Make Love Like A Man', 'Armageddon It', 'Have You Ever Needed Someone So Bad', 'Rock Of Ages', 'Hysteria', 'Bringin' On The Heartbreak'

Japanese tracklisting: 'Pour Some Sugar On Me' (Historia Video Edit), 'Photograph', 'Love Bites', 'Let's Get Rocked', 'Two Steps Behind' (Acoustic Version), 'Animal', 'Action', 'Rocket' (Visualize Video Edit), 'When Love & Hate Collide', 'Rock! Rock! (Till You Drop)', 'Armageddon It', 'Foolin'', 'Have You Ever Needed Someone So Bad', 'Rock Of Ages', 'Hysteria', 'Bringin' On The Heartbreak', 'Can't Keep Away From The Flame' (Previously Unreleased)

Bonus Live CD: 'Let's Get Rocked', 'Armageddon It', 'Foolin'', 'Rocket', 'Two Steps Behind', 'Pour Some Sugar On Me', 'Rock Of Ages', 'Love Bites', 'Photograph'

Leppard's first greatest hits compilation was also its richest, gathering up the standout tracks from their most successful years. Singles from every previous album except *On Through The Night* were included. Where a track had been re-edited for single release, the single's edit was used, rather than the original album track.

The collection included one new track, 'When Love & Hate Collide', a leftover from the *Adrenalize* sessions. It went 5x platinum in the US and platinum in the UK. The collection also included the previously unreleased track 'Can't Keep Away From The Flame'.

'When Love & Hate Collide' (Elliott/Savage)

Released as a single on 2 October 1995

Charts: US *Billboard* Hot 100: 58; UK Singles: 2

Produced between *Adrenalize* and *Slang*, this Elliott/Savage collaboration was one of Leppard's most successful singles at home, reaching number two on the UK Singles chart. Intended for *Adrenalize*, its demo incarnation featured the last guitar solo Steve Clark ever recorded.

A typically heavy ballad, the song breathes in its verses, giving Elliott space to make his plea to a woman he's fallen out with, but rather than pining, he's determined to set the conflict aside. It's not an original theme for Leppard, but it conveys a greater maturity and patience than previous takes; the harmonies and Collen's clean, gentle lead add to the song's emotional depth. Orchestral strings are layered into the mix, heightening the song's sense of anticipation.

'Can't Keep Away From The Flame' (Elliott/Collen)

Bonus track on the Japanese edition of the *Vault* compilation album

Recorded in the basement of Rick Savage's home in Dublin, this track recalls an earlier time – the sometimes-folkish pop/rock days of Leppard's youth, when bands like Crosby, Stills & Nash, Fairport Convention and Fleetwood Mac in their post-Peter Green, pre-Lindsey/Stevie days often leaned acoustic. The tune is sparse – just a pair of acoustic guitars, Elliott's lead vocal and a single harmony voice – but the reading is earnest and articulate. Little-known even to die-hard Leppard fans, it is, in fact, an exceptional tune. Collen's acoustic lead work is stand-out.

Best Of Def Leppard (2004)

Disc One: 'Pour Some Sugar On Me' (Historia Video Edit), 'Photograph', 'Love Bites', 'Let's Get Rocked', 'Two Steps Behind', 'Animal', 'Heaven Is', 'Rocket' (Visualize Video Edit), 'When Love & Hate Collide', 'Action', 'Long, Long Way To Go', 'Make Love Like A Man', 'Armageddon It', 'Have You Ever Needed Someone So Bad', 'Rock Of Ages', 'Hysteria', 'Bringin' On The Heartbreak'

Disc Two: 'Rock! Rock! (Till You Drop)', 'Waterloo Sunset', 'Promises', 'Slang', 'Foolin'', 'Now', 'Rock Brigade', 'Women', 'Let It Go', 'Too Late For Love', 'High 'N' Dry (Saturday Night)', 'Work It Out', 'Billy's Got A Gun' (Edited Version), 'Another Hit And Run', 'Stand Up (Kick Love Into Motion)', 'Wasted', 'Die Hard The Hunter'

The *Best Of* compilation extended *Vault* (Disc One is the entire UK release) with the addition of 'Long Long Way To Go' from the *X* album. All tracks on this collection were the album versions with the exceptions of 'Pour Some Sugar on Me' (video edit version), 'Rocket' (single edit) and a slightly shorter mix of 'Bringin' On The Heartbreak'. Also included was a cover of The Kinks' 'Waterloo Sunset', which would be included on the *Yeah!* album two years later. *Best Of* went platinum in the UK.

Rock Of Ages: The Definitive Collection (2005)

Disc One: 'Pour Some Sugar On Me' (Historia Video Edit), 'Photograph', 'Love Bites', 'Let's Get Rocked', 'Two Steps Behind' (Acoustic Version), 'Animal', 'Heaven Is', 'Foolin'', 'Rocket' (Visualize Video Edit), 'When Love & Hate Collide', 'Armageddon It', 'Have You Ever Needed Someone So Bad', 'Rock Of Ages',

'Hysteria', 'Miss You In A Heartbeat' (Acoustic Version), 'Bringin' On The Heartbreak', 'Switch 625'
Disc Two: 'Rock! Rock! (Till You Drop)', 'Let It Go', 'High 'N' Dry (Saturday Night)', 'Too Late For Love', 'No Matter What', 'Promises', 'Mirror, Mirror (Look Into My Eyes)', 'Women', 'Another Hit And Run', 'Slang', 'Stand Up (Kick Love Into Motion)', 'Rock Brigade', 'Now', 'Paper Sun', 'Work It Out', 'Die Hard The Hunter', 'Wasted', 'Billy's Got A Gun' (Edited Version)
Released a year later, this compilation was a North American version of *Best Of*. The track order was different, and included the Badfinger cover 'No Matter What' (to be released later on *Yeah!*) in place of 'Waterloo Sunset'. The full-length version of 'Bringin' On The Heartbreak' was used. The album went platinum in the US.

The Lost Session (2018)
Disc One: 'Let It Go', 'Rock On', 'Foolin'', 'Promises', 'When Love & Hate Collide', 'Bringin' On The Heartbreak'
Recorded in 2006, this brief collection was recorded for exclusive release on Apple Music services and its iTunes store, but a royalty dispute between the band and Universal Music Group delayed the release.

The Story So Far – The Best Of (2018)
Disc One: 'Animal', 'Photograph', 'Pour Some Sugar On Me', 'Love Bites', 'Let's Get Rocked', 'Armageddon It', 'Foolin'', 'Two Steps Behind', 'Heaven Is', 'Rocket', 'Hysteria', 'Have You Ever Needed Someone So Bad', 'Make Love Like A Man', 'Action', 'When Love & Hate Collide', 'Rock Of Ages', 'Personal Jesus'
Disc Two: 'Let's Go', 'Promises', 'Slang', 'Bringin' On The Heartbreak', 'Rock On' (Radio Remix), 'Nine Lives' (With Tim McGraw), 'Work It Out', 'Stand Up (Kick Love Into Motion)', 'Dangerous', 'Now', 'Undefeated', 'Tonight', 'C'mon C'mon', 'Man Enough', 'No Matter What', 'All I Want Is Everything', 'It's All About Believin'', 'Kings Of The World'
Vinyl Bonus Single: 'We All Need Christmas'
This compilation included all tracks from *Vault* except 'Miss You In A Heartbeat' and added tracks from *Songs From The Sparkle Lounge* and *Def Leppard*. The studio tracks from *Mirror Ball* were also included. The album went gold in the UK.

Drastic Symphonies (2023)
'Turn To Dust', 'Paper Sun', 'Animal', 'Pour Some Sugar On Me', 'Hysteria', 'Love Bites', 'Goodbye For Good This Time', 'Love', 'Gods Of War', 'Angels (Can't Help You Now)', 'Bringin' On The Heartbreak', 'Switch 625', 'Have You Ever Needed Someone So Bad', 'Too Late For Love', 'When Love & Hate Collide', 'Kings Of The World'
This album uses the vocal tracks from the original recordings, backed by orchestral accompaniment from the Royal Philharmonic Orchestra (recorded

at Abbey Road, no less). The rock press praised the final product, as exemplified by Gary Graff's positive feedback for *Ultimate Classic Rock*: 'The results are unquestionably intriguing and fresh – a genuinely new way of approaching these tracks.'

Stand-out moments include Elliott duetting his own lead vocal on 'Too Late For Love'; tense strings replacing the guitars on 'Gods Of War', making the atmosphere of the already-dark tune even more ominous; a counterintuitive twist on 'Animal', wherein a lush new intro and soaring strings place the song's energy exclusively in Elliott's lead vocal and the backing harmonies, to surprising effect; a stirring take on 'Love Bites' in which Steve Clark's original guitar solo plays against the orchestral backing; and the somewhat controversial revision of 'Pour Some Sugar On Me', in which Elliott duets with Emm Gryner to piano accompaniment, altering the tone of the song completely.

The album went to number four on the UK Albums chart, number one on the UK Rock & Metal Albums chart and number 54 on the US *Billboard* 200.

Box Sets

The Collection: Volume One (2018)

On Through The Night, High 'N' Dry, Pyromania, Hysteria, Live At The La Forum 1983, Rarities Volume One, The Def Leppard EP

This box set gathers together their first EP and the first four studio albums, along with a live concert recorded in Los Angeles and a disc of rare tracks.

The Collection: Volume Two (2019)

Adrenalize, Retro Active, Slang, Euphoria, Rarities Volume Two, Rarities Volume Three, Rarities Volume Four

This second box set volume continues to archive the band's studio albums through 1999, along with three more discs of rarities and their first compilation album.

The Early Years 79-81 (2020)

On Through The Night, High 'N' Dry, When The Walls Came Tumbling Down – Live In Oxford 26/04/1980, Too Many Jitterbugs – B-Sides And Rarities, Raw – Early BBC Recordings

A boon for collectors, this set recycles the first two studio albums, along with a live concert from 1980 and recordings of early BBC appearances. A disc of early B-sides and additional rarities is also included.

The Collection: Volume Three (2021)

X, Yeah!, Songs From The Sparkle Lounge, B-Sides, Yeah! II (bonus album of cover songs), *Yeah! Live!* (live album of cover songs)

This volume includes the first three studio albums post-2000, as well as a second album of cover tracks and a live concert from the *Yeah!* tour.

Sources/Bibliography

Magazine/Newspaper Sources

'Brian May's Effusive Def Leppard Rock Hall Induction Speech', *Rolling Stone,* 30 March 2019.
'Def Leppard: Getting On With It and Getting It On', Louisville *Courier-Journal,* 22 November 1992.
'Def Leppard: To Hell & Back', *Rolling Stone,* 30 April 1992.
Hysteria review, Louisville *Courier-Journal,* April 1987.
Jim Steinman interview, *Melody Maker,* 1989.

Book Sources

Collen, P., with Epting, C., *Adrenalized: Life, Def Leppard, And Beyond* (Atria, 2015).
Elliott, P., *Def Leppard: The Early Years 79 – 81* (Mercury, 2020).
Fricke, D., with Haflin, R., *Animal Instinct* (Zomba Books, 1987).
Gill, J., *Leppard Tracks: Def Leppard On Tour Volume 1, 1978-1988* (LeppardTracks, 2008-2018).
Kenning, T., *My Time With Def Leppard And Other Bands* (Independently published, 2019).

Internet Sources

www.songfacts.com
https://www.rollingstone.com/music/music-lists/def-leppards-joe-elliott-my-life-in-15-songs-78460/high-n-dry-saturday-night-1981-162796/
https://www.goldminemag.com/articles/def-leppards-guitarist-phil-collen-offers-track-track-review-hysteria

Video Sources

Def Leppard: Hysteria, Classic Albums, 2002